MW00884592

The Realities of Human Trafficking

From the Inside Out to Freedom

Ruth Rondon

Copyright © 2016 Ruth Rondon
The Realities of Human Trafficking from the Inside Out to Freedom

All rights reserved under International and
Pan American Copyright Law, including the
right of reproduction in whole or in part,
without the written permission of the publisher.
Requests for such permission should be addressed to
Ruth Rondon at ruthsurvived@gmail.com

Manufactured in the United States of America

9 8 7 6 5 4 3 2 1

First Edition

Printed in the United States of America

ISBN 978-1530975631

Acknowledgements

This book was written with love for all my family and future generations. I hope my book helps you see how the cycle of abuse continues. I hope my book helps you see how you can prevent the cycle of abuse and live with love and understanding.

Please:
- Listen to our children and listen to what they are not saying. *Just because there is not a collision doesn't mean they are not hurting. Just because you don't see tears, does not mean they are not in pain.*
- Apologize and forgive. You won't regret it.
- If someone treats you like shit, remember there is something wrong with them, not you. Normal people don't go around abusing other human beings.
- Have heart-to-heart talks. Don't walk around the elephant in the room when you know there are issues that need to be addressed. Find a way, a time and a place to talk about sensitive issues. You can **live** life to the fullest by addressing sensitive issues as they come. Don't let it fester.
- Remember to accept love from others as well as extend it to others.
- Don't take life too seriously. Give yourself a break and laugh out loud

I will forever be thankful to my brothers and sisters for taking me back, after all I put them through. Thank you so much for being my role models and trail blazers. I don't know what would have become of me without your forgiveness. I will forever cherish the good times we had. We have been quite a team, haven't we? (smile)

Thank you Mom for all you've done for me. I know how hard it was for you here on earth. I will forever be indebted to you for all your sacrifices. Putting your life on the line for me is a love beyond the call of duty. You are truly my hero.

I want to thank my dear friends (ex co-workers) for being the greatest friends and co-workers anyone could ever ask for. I kept a secret from so many for so long and when I opened up to you, you honored that secret and it means the world to me. You will never know. Thank you so much.

I want to thank my book editors Natalie Hart, Russ Johnson, Laurie Johnson and Betty Navis for all the time and work spent on editing my book. Going through my life with me has been such a gift. Your knowledge and skills are invaluable. Thank you so much.

It has been a great experience to work with Gary Hoffman from JDI Apollo Graphic Communications in designing my book. Your expertise and hard work is greatly appreciated.

I want to thank my Christian counselor Ken Navis and his wife Betty Navis for believing in me, all the way. Your loving kindness and faith has left an impact on me and my life that I will forever be thankful for.

I want to thank Char Fouty for staying with me in my time of need. People who stand by those in need and put their own fears aside for the sake of another are those of true grit. Thank you for demonstrating to me what love for our neighbor is really all about.

I want to thank Russ and Laurie Johnson for all they have done for me. We are bonded forever. I love you both very much. The love you have for each other is proof that marriage can be full of love when God is in the center. Others love to be around you because of your strong faith. God bless you both. Thank you so much for helping me write my book and seeing it through to the end.

I want to thank Lorilyn Wiering and all the folks at Red Cord Community and all the friends of RCC for believing in me and encouraging me to tell my story and also for demonstrating to me how to love others and also how to practice self care. Your faith in me has lifted me higher than you will know. You helped me to discover my voice, realize my strengths and helped me gain even more freedom to be me. Thank you so much for all your help in writing my book.

I want to thank my employers for knowing my history and hiring me anyway and giving me a second chance.

I want to thank the folks at the YWCA West Central Michigan for all you do.

I want to thank my therapist, Patty Haist, the clinical director at the YWCA West Central Michigan, for teaching me what I need to learn about myself, trauma and PTSD. Thank you for your patience, knowledge and your calming presence.

I want to thank the kind Christian detective. Your kindness will never be forgotten. I know you wanted justice for me, and that alone left a huge impact on me. I know the shame culture and stigma you were up against.

I want to thank Senator Judy Emmons for recommending me for the MICHIGAN HUMAN TRAFFICKNG HEALTH ADVISORY BOARD. I am so glad I wrote to you about how important it is to me that human trafficking victims and survivors are represented. You are a true leader who fights for what she believes in. With women like you I stand strong.

I want to thank Senator Emmon's Chief of Staff Laura Toy for all her support and for being who she is. You have opened doors of opportunity for me and I thank you.

I want to thank Patti Hathaway for giving me a co-authoring opportunity to create the www.humantraffickingelearning.com with you. It has been great working with you. We held each up during the difficult times and shared a lot of laughs during the good times. I will be forever grateful to you.

I want to thank the folks at the University of Michigan Human Trafficking Law Clinic for all the hard work they put into helping victims and survivors of human trafficking.

I want to give a special thanks to Suellyn Scarnecchia, clinical professor of law at the University of Michigan Human Trafficking Law Clinic for her professionalism and commitment to helping others find freedom.

To my dear friend Gail Warren:

Thank you for being there for me when I need you. You and I have become like family and I want you to know I will always love you. Neither time, nor distance will ever break the bond we share. No matter how much time goes by and no matter the distance between us, we just pick up from where we left off. I am so blessed to have you in my life. Thank you for all your encouragement and straight forward talk. You help me see my emotional blind spots in a very loving and gentle way.

Most of all, I thank God for His never changing love. I thank God for taking care of me when I wasn't even taking care of myself and for sending me all the caring people that crossed my path, who believed in me and who left an impact on me with their kind words, for staying with me in my mess, and loving me unconditionally.

"We need to teach our daughters how to distinguish between a man who flatters her and a man who compliments her; a man who spends money on her and a man who invests in her; a man who views her as property and a man who views her properly; a man who lusts after her and a man who loves her; a man who believes he is God's gift to women and a man who remembers that women are gifts from God."

Anonymous

Table of Contents

Some names and identifying details have been changed to protect the privacy of individuals.

I have tried to recreate events, locales and conversations from my memories of them. In order to maintain their anonymity in some instances I have changed the names of individuals and places, I may have changed some identifying characteristics and details such as physical properties, occupations and places.

INTRODUCTION

Most people don't want to hear about commercial sexual exploitation, rape, or post-traumatic stress disorder (PTSD), but you picked up this book for a reason. You may have fallen prey to the sex trade and are looking for hope by reading how another got out. You may be a survivor who is still reliving the traumas. You may know someone who has been raped or trafficked whom you are trying to understand. If so, you need to know that you or your loved one *can* overcome sexual abuse and/or sex trafficking.

My wish is that this book gives you hope.

I am sixty-one years old now. I recently retired from a white-collar job I maintained for twenty-three years, but for eighteen years before that I was drug-addicted and sexually exploited, dragged into that life after a childhood of being abused, of witnessing abuse, and of being raped.

When I was little, I couldn't fathom the magnitude of the crimes committed against me. I was preyed upon by so many people. The abuse I was subjected to led to an adult life of even more abuse, self-destruction, bad choices, and poor decisions.

It took a long time for me to finally be able to wrap my head around the fact that I actually did survive it all. For years, I totally disregarded the fact that I was alive (proof that I'd survived). My thoughts were focused on the traumas and the horrors alone. I couldn't get past them. Intrusive thoughts hindered me from being able to feel any joy and kept me from seeing any purpose to my life. Fear was my constant companion. I would have good days—but then that whisper inside me wouldn't let me forget.

To others I appeared to be fine, but I am a survivor of abuse, of rape, of shame, of drug addiction and commercial sexual exploitation. I truly am a survivor. Today I'm learning to embrace my survival and live fully every day, instead of dying every day, like I did for so long.

My wish is that my book helps you to understand either yourself, or someone you love, better.

I wrote down every trauma I had been through. Reliving the trauma is what victims do, over and over again, anyway, so I wasn't looking forward to writing it all down. As I wrote, I felt the fear and terror as if it was happening all over again. I wrote down all the details of each trauma to the end.

I had to step away from my computer after each one, to break down and cry it out. When I couldn't cry anymore, it was then that I was able to embrace all of the many blessings in my life. It had been daunting, but writing about each trauma and sorting through the lowest points in my life is what helped me heal. I looked around my home, saw my cat and all the comforts of my home, and I was able to stop reliving it. I was able to bring myself out of the darkness, back to the present moment, and now I can see the light, because it's over! It's truly over!

After writing, I discovered the freedom I had been longing for. I was finally able to tuck the sadness away into history, once and for all, and embrace my survival. All those traumas had become just stories when put on paper. The power the trauma and shame had over me was released.

In *The Courage to Heal*, Ellen Bass and Laura Davis write, "So often survivors have had their experiences denied, trivialized, or distorted. Writing is an important avenue for healing because it gives you the opportunity to define your own reality. You can say: This did happen to me. It was that bad. It was the fault and responsibility of the adult. I was—and am—innocent."

Make no mistake about it: no little girl grows up wanting to be pimped out. They are usually victims of some kind of abuse as children long before they are victims of trafficking. That's certainly my story, and if it's your story, too, I hope reading about my path and what it taught me will help you begin to make sense of your path.

If it's the story of someone you love, I believe you will benefit from hearing my story of survival. For non-survivors it is not easy to hear the words "I was raped" or "I was abused." It's easy to immediately go into denial, become defensive, panic, or offer pity – none of which help the survivor, and none of which help you understand the survivor you love. I want to empower friends and family — and even the larger community — to embrace survivors with love and understanding.

My wish is that my book is part of breaking the cycle of abuse.

There is so much secrecy around child abuse, rape, and sex trafficking. Secrets eat away at us and make it possible for abuse to become a cycle that continues from generation to generation. Someone has to step up to break the secrecy, to break the cycle.

By writing this book, I'm doing my part. I'm stepping up. I broke the secrecy of abuse in my own life and I'm passing on what I've learned, in hopes that others will tell their own stories, break their own cycles, and pass on what they've learned.

Even though I didn't detail all my traumas in this book, my story may be hard for some to read. I want you to know I am with you with your pain. There's a lot of sadness in my book, but understanding why bad things happened to me might just keep them from happening in the future to someone else—that is why I work so hard to understand. I encourage you to work hard to understand the sadness in your own life. Understanding moves us forward, and helps us break the cycle of abuse.

I know there are others out there who need to know the power they hold within themselves, to know that they aren't alone, to know how to trace their life's events and understand how their relationships lead to the mess they are or were in.

My wish is that my book points to lasting hope.

Lasting hope means not just surviving the trauma, but moving past it to forgiveness – forgiving yourself and forgiving others. When I recognized the PTSD symptoms in my parents, I acquired compassion for them, and was able to lower my expectations of them. I was then able to let go of the hurt and rage I held inside for so long.

I don't claim to be an expert on parenting. I don't even have any children. I can only tell you what was missing in my childhood and what resulted from it.

After living through years of secrecy and abuse, I finally got it: I am worthy of more.

You are, too.

Let me say that again. You are worth being rescued. Worth being saved, heard, listened to, and healed. It's all possible.

I survived for a reason. Maybe writing this book is one reason.

CHAPTER ONE

My Story

I was lying on a gurney at the ER with no idea what was going on. I was alone for a very long time and it was very cold in there. The healthcare workers on the other side of the curtain were venting their frustrations to each other because an ambulance had just brought in a very belligerent thirteen-year-old girl. She was kicking and screaming and wouldn't talk to anybody.

That little girl was me.

The police came in to talk to me and they probed me for information but all I could do was stare at the ceiling. No one had explained anything to me and I didn't dare ask, either. I could feel their disdain and I was so afraid of what they were going to do.

The only hospital I knew of back then was the one downtown and I assumed that's where we were, so it added to my confusion when the police said they'd take me downtown if I didn't talk. To me, downtown didn't mean jail, it meant Steketee's department store. It was Christmastime and I thought maybe the police were thinking it would be good for me to see the Christmas puppets in

Steketee's window. Offering me a chance to go see the puppets reinforced my belief that the cops were on my side, my heroes.

I said, "Yes. Take me downtown."

I longed for them to hear me out but I was even more afraid of what they would do if they knew I'd been at a beer party and that I had sex with two grown men there who persuaded me to go to the back yard with them.

I'll never forget how I laid there on the cold grass, stiff with fear, while they took turns on me. They were not gentle and I prayed it would be over soon. You see, I thought it was my fault that I was raped.

———————

It all started when I was ten years old. My sister and friends and I were hanging out at a mall and having a good time. A stranger lured me away; he seemed nice, at first, and not too many people were nice to me back then. I was taught at home and in school to do as I was told and to behave. I did as I was told that day, and I did behave. He raped me.

No one had ever sat me down and taught me anything about sex. I had never even seen a man naked before. I couldn't make sense of any of this. I felt so dirty.

When I got home I showed mother my bloody underwear and told her what happened.

It took a lot of courage for me to tell my mom what happened, but my courage was not rewarded. My mother said I was a whore and my father beat me. I concluded that I must be the guilty one.

Mom told me to get in the bathtub and scrub the dirt off me. I sat in the tub, fully clothed, crying all afternoon while she walked back and forth past the bathroom door, telling me I would never be any good and that I should be ashamed of myself. She came in the bathroom once and placed a feminine pad and belt on the shelf and told me to put them on. I had no idea how to use either one of them.

Dad thought the only way to punish us for misbehaving and for not doing what we were told to do was to beat us. Mom believed the only way to teach us was by humiliating us.

After that day, Mother acted like it never happened. It was like she was telling me that we had to cover it up with a sugar coating and bury it under a cover of hypocrisy.

My brother's buddy preyed on us kids after my two older brothers went to fight in the Vietnam War in 1966. I was about twelve years old when he approached us as we were cutting through a field one day, on our way home from hanging out at the bowling alley. I always wanted to be in the crowd my brother was in; be accepted. I didn't realize his very murky intentions so I went along with him too. He led me into his parents' house and raped me. I did as I was told that day, too.

I didn't resist but I didn't cooperate either. How can a child cooperate with an adult act they don't understand? I remember my body was stiff from the fear and the extreme violation I was experiencing. He was gentler with me than the first man was though. He said he could tell that I enjoyed it. This added to my confusion and I concluded I was supposed to have liked it.

(This was hard for me to write but you need to know what pedophiles and child rapists say to their victims so you'll know to what degree of confusion the child experiences after being raped. If I had had a trusted go-to-person in my life I could have asked that person questions about my feelings and what he said.)

Children want to do what they are supposed to do. How

was I to know what I was supposed to do or how I was supposed to feel? No one ever taught me anything about sex, dating or puberty; on what was appropriate or inappropriate or on what was normal and what wasn't. I was forced to make my own conclusions. I had no one in my life I could go to with my questions either. What do we expect from our children when we fail them so miserably?

Failing our children like this is no different than an employer expecting an employee to do the job without ever training them. Many employers tell their staff that the company has an open door policy and "if you have any concerns at all, feel free to let us know. "With an open door policy employees feel safe to express themselves and ask questions. But we don't do this with our children. This needs to change.

Because of what happened last time, I didn't tell anyone. I was afraid I'd be slapped or beaten again, and I didn't want my family to be humiliated by me. I was convinced that there's something terribly wrong with ME.

I tried to forget it ever happened, but since it happened to me before, I began to think this was what growing up was supposed to be like. I thought all kids had to go through this. I even wondered if my brother had anything to do with it. After all, it was Ken's buddy.

So when it happened again at age thirteen, and the police and healthcare workers treated me like my mother had, like I was just "being bad," it only reinforced the feelings of shame and insecurity the rapes had caused.

I was so ashamed. I couldn't look anyone in the face. No matter what, I didn't want my parents to find out because it would only reinforce their belief that I was just a whore. Again, I'd done what I was told, which was what they'd raised me to do, but I was too afraid to admit to anyone that I had cooperated.

This had all started because my sister and neighborhood friends went to a beer party. We just wanted to have fun. I didn't mean to cause any trouble for anybody.

The police got angrier with me because I had agreed to go downtown with them. They thought I was being a smart aleck, so they gave up on me. They left! It was so hard to watch my heroes walk out on me.

When the hospital diagnosed me with syphilis, they treated me as though it was my fault, like I must have asked for it. They never even asked who could have done this to me! What else could I conclude: I must be the guilty one, beyond redemption. I thought I was a disgusting child and I wanted to hide my disgusting self from the world. I wanted to die.

———•———

Later in life I learned that a person can go years without symptoms of syphilis, which means I could very well have contracted the disease from the first rape, when I was ten years old. Later in life, realizing the severe neglect I was subjected to was hard for me to accept. By the time I realized that it was not my fault what could I do? I was so angry and didn't know what to do with that anger for a long time. It took years to be able to finally let it go.

Studies have shown that when a person is left to process a rape or a sexual assault all on their own, they will most likely develop PTSD and they will blame and shame themselves for it—and it's ten times worse for children. Sexual abuse and rape is shaming for women and men, girls and boys. Shame is a self-worth injury. If these injuries are not professionally addressed the injury may not heal correctly, which can put the victim on a dark and lonely path of self-destruction. It's a downward spiral of overwhelming and unnecessary shame. That's what PTSD is.

This is what happened to me. I think it should be called Post Traumatic SHAME Disorder.

We didn't know as much about trauma back then. Today, we

recognize that an STD in a young child is a sign of rape, and can be a sign of sex trafficking. Children cannot consent to sex. Sex without consent is rape. Studies show that children who are abused and neglected often develop a victim mindset and it's this mindset that traffickers prey upon.

Today it is understood that being subjected to ongoing trauma, **without support,** can result in toxic stress. Dr. Bruce Perry, M.D., Ph.D. Founder of Child Trauma Academy says that even if children **are** subjected to ongoing trauma, toxic stress can be avoided if they have a good support system or have good relational health. Ongoing trauma and relational poverty together, can result in a child out of control. Once a tolerance to a chronically stressful environment is built up, even a tiny dose of stress can raise stress levels and you have an out of control child. (See references).

Sexual, physical and emotional abuse in childhood serves as boot camp for prostitution in that it normalizes the abuse that is so common in the trade. (See references).

The hospital called my behavior a nervous breakdown and sent me back home.

Mom was angry that I'd been at a beer party. My actions were a reflection on her and I'd embarrassed her, once again.

My parents were separated at the time. They would separate many times before they finally divorced. The divorce was granted 1969 when long separations were required and grounds for divorce had to be proven.

Dad came to the house. I was eager to see him because even after all the beatings, I had a fantasy belief that he was a super hero. Many kids develop a fantasy world about their missing parent because it's difficult for them to face the harsh truth that some parents aren't capable of being good parents. It's an even harsher truth that some parents don't even want to learn how to be good parents.

But Dad didn't come to the house to see me. From the bedroom I could hear him argue with Mom about whose fault it was that I was such a mess. He then came to the bedroom to say good-bye.

Mother said she was disgusted with me because I was full of filthy diseases. I couldn't understand why I was even born. I believed everyone could live in so much more peace if I was dead.

———•———

To adults, it seems logical to avoid situations that have caused embarrassment or shame before, but children have a disproportionate need for nurturing and love, which makes them too trusting and very vulnerable. Children want to behave, but if they are never taught, they don't know what the rules are, what the laws are, or what's appropriate or inappropriate. They just know what they feel. Their decision to comply with the manipulations of their abuser is based on their emotions, not from logic or reason.

Loving relationships were foreign in our house. My parents and grandparents never took the time to understand any of us kids. The rule of thumb was: Children are to be seen and not heard. If we were to ever know what a loving relationship looked and felt like, we had to figure it out on our own. It took a long, long time.

CHAPTER TWO

Is There A Loving World Out There?

The day after the chaotic event at the hospital mother pinched the top of my ear as she steered me into the car to go to the Health Department to be treated for syphilis.

While in the waiting room I tried to rest my head on her arm, but she shoved me away and wouldn't let me touch her — more evidence that I was a piece of shit.

I was told to lie on my stomach on the clinic bed. They treated me as though I was a very bad girl.

They pulled my pants down and I sobbed and sobbed. The nurse stabbed my cheek with a needle. She gave no warning, offered no apologies, and showed no sympathy. I screamed as they held me down. They didn't even give me any privacy; I saw a lady in the waiting room watching the whole thing.

We got back in the car again and drove for several miles. I thought we were going to see a doctor about the bumps on my head, but when we pulled into the long, winding driveway, I realized we were at a mental institution.

"What are we doing here? Do they have doctors here?"

She reassured me it was just a physical exam.

A doctor showed me a picture of a man looking down at a naked woman on a bed with a sheet over her, and asked me to make up a story about it.

The story I made up was, "He had just raped her." That was the most anyone ever got out of me about the rapes at that time. It was never brought up again, not by the folks at Pine Rest, by anyone at home, nor by my neighborhood buddies.

We were asked to have a seat in the waiting room after they did their physiological testing. After waiting for a very long hour, someone beckoned Mother to the exit door. Two intimidating-looking men entered the waiting room from the other side. One of them took me by the hand and led me in the opposite direction of Mother. I didn't know what was going on. As I was led away and as she walked out, I begged Mother not to leave me there. I sobbed and screamed, but she kept on walking. She never even looked back. I can still remember the sound of the door closing behind her. She was gone.

I couldn't believe it! My biggest fears were coming true. I was being abandoned. My mother was gone and I was now under the jurisdiction of these men.

CHAPTER THREE

You Call This Help?

It takes a Community to Raise a Child
It takes a Community to Fail a Child

They put me in what they called a quiet room: a padded cell with a mattress on the floor. I ate and slept there for seven days. I was so heavily medicated, and it was such a long time ago, that I only remember people coming in to poke my butt with a medication now and then and to bring me food. All this trauma and confusion convinced me that I was dumped off because I was so bad.

I resigned myself to the fact that that's just what people do with bad kids: they get rid of them

One day a staff member took a group of us girls with her to the basement for some reason. I wandered off away from the group and noticed there was a room. I looked inside. In the middle of the room was a gurney. My mind went back to when I was on a gurney at the hospital, but in this room there were long and short, sharp knives and some kind of hatchets hanging on the walls. There were also aprons that looked like they were made of rubber. It felt very eerie to me.

I asked the staff lady what the room was and she said, "That's where autopsies are done." I had bad dreams about that room after that. I always wondered if I would end up in that room one day.

Healthcare professionals need to understand that medical equipment can be intimidating and scary for a child.

Once I was in with the general population of the adolescent unit, Dad tried to get in to see me several times, but they wouldn't let him in. I was so mad; I cried and cried. I blamed Pine Rest for ruining my chance to be with my dad without Mother fighting with him. I felt like my dad and I longed to be together, but something always foiled it.

In reality, I was the only one doing the longing. Mom and Dad were waging a bitter custody battle against one another, and I was thrown in the middle of their angry politics. His attempted visit at Pine Rest was probably another maneuver on his part to prove my mother wrong or at fault.

My brother Don and his wife came to visit me. It seemed to me that they shook their heads in disgust at everything I said—disgust in me. This reconfirmed to me that I was the scum of the earth.

By now, whenever anyone shook their head I interpreted it as, "they are repulsed by me." I took this complex with me into adulthood. Even in adulthood I analyzed facial expressions, always looking for one of approval. I couldn't easily blow off an expression of disapproval because of the low opinion I had of myself. I was preoccupied with what others thought of me. Approval was like a high for me. I sought it out for even just a few seconds of instant gratification.

As part of my counseling, at every appointment with my psychiatrist, I was injected with what the girls in the adolescent unit called "truth serum."

As I was led to his office for the first time, I expected to be molested. I wasn't sure by whom yet though. Maybe the staff who was leading me down the hallway? By then, I had come to fear authority figures, so when I found myself alone with one, I intended to be a good girl and do what was expected of me. I thought satisfying men's sexual desires was what was expected of me.

From my seat in his regal-looking office, I noticed the awards and certificates displayed on the walls. These framed documents told me he was more important than me and more believable, too. I suspected he was the one who I would service sexually.

The door was closed and there were no windows. It was the perfect setting for him to get away with molesting or raping me. It gave him the privacy he needed and it made me feel powerless. It was just me and him.

After the injection, he looked me in the face as if he was waiting for me to say or do something. I wasn't sure if I was supposed to initiate the sex act or if he would. He kept looking in my face. "What am I suppose to be doing?" I wondered. I considered reaching for his zipper to unzip his pants but he wasn't in a good sitting position for that either. I wanted him to know that I intended to be a good girl. I didn't want him to get mad at me. I didn't know what to do or say so I said, "I love you." His face turned to the look of confusion. I was just as confused as he was.

I don't remember any more details about this incident but he never molested me or tried anything. As time went on I saw him as a good guy but not very understanding.

I know now that he was probably looking in my eyes to see whether the drug had taken affect yet, but no one explained any procedures to me at the time. If I had known what to expect, it may have helped my fears subside. And if I had been reassured that he wasn't expecting anything from me, I may have opened up to him more than I did.

When I think back on this and consider what healthcare professionals can do today, I imagine that he could have looked me in the face with warm eyes and a warm and accepting smile and said, "Ruth, you don't have to say that. You don't have to say or do anything at all. I'm not expecting anything from you. I'm here to help *you*."

It is very difficult for me to write about this incident, but it's important to realize how vulnerable our kids are. This kind of vulnerability can be too tempting for some not take advantage of. We need to empower our children so they can protect themselves, but we also need to make sure we know who we are entrusting our children with.

Hospitals, clinics, police departments, schools, rehabs and safe houses need to have policies set into place so the one-on-ones between doctors and patients, teachers and students, police officers and suspects, victims and advocates are monitored or at least documented to make those in authority positions accountable. If predators that are in positions of authority don't have to answer to anyone, to them, this is an ideal position to be in. They look for positions like this so they can be close to the vulnerable, so they can do as they please during a one-on-one. Remember the advocate, the police officer, the counselor, the preacher that you talk with may not be the well intentioned person they make out to be.

———•———

One day, at Pine Rest, a bus drove from building to building and picked everyone up who was going to the occupational therapy class. It was a pottery class and it sounded cool. I was excited about getting out and doing something, but when I saw who was on the bus, I freaked out: it was full of mental patients who were drooling and making weird noises. They scared me, but the staff woman made me get on the bus.

As I scanned the bus, looking for a seat, a mental patient reached out to me. I turned around to make a run for it, but the staff woman behind me nudged me to keep on going and said, sternly, "Don't hold up the line, Ruth."

She obviously wasn't concerned with whether I felt safe or not. This reinforced my belief that the folks at Pine Rest couldn't be trusted.

I enjoyed the class, but I dreaded going to any other classes, if it required getting on the bus.

If I had been given choices I would have at least felt like my feelings mattered, but I was expected to follow the schedule at Pine Rest, obey and do as I was told or I'd be punished, which is just how mom and dad brought me up. I stayed in my victim mentality.

Sue Grossman, in "Offering Children Choices: Encouraging Autonomy and Learning While Minimizing Conflicts," states that children who do not develop autonomy are liable to remain dependent on adults or to be overly influenced by peers. That certainly held true for me.

I figured I was worthless, so I simply rebelled at everything and rejected everyone at Pine Rest. I'm sure some of the methods they used back then are not used today, but they never even tried to help me combat my belief that there was something wrong with me.

I can't say it was all bad there. There were some loving staff people. Some seemed to want to understand, but I didn't feel understood. I felt I was dumped off there because I was bad. Over and over again, I asked why I had to be there and they only told me it was for my own good. The only conclusion I came up with is that I must be tainted with some kind of contamination.

Mother attended some counseling sessions with me, but she never said much. She sat in her chair with her arms folded and was very resistant and defensive.

Although we never followed through, another girl and I planned to run away when we had the chance. We intended to depend on what she called "johns," men who paid for sexual favors. She told me stories of how easy it was to get money by selling herself. It sounded so easy.

CHAPTER FOUR

Prey For Everyone

I recently retrieved my records from Pine Rest. My discharge cites: "Home continues to be a severe problem in that it is a very unhealthy situation in that she has a fair amount of contact with an alcoholic father and we refuse to discharge her to this home setting."

Even though Pine Rest didn't want to send me back home, nine months after being left there, I had to go back for financial reasons. I remember how low the ceilings seemed at home; the ceilings at Pine Rest were very high.

Although it was home, everything seemed foreign to me. It was a big adjustment, but nobody guided me through it. I had to find a way to preserve a sense of trust in people who were untrustworthy, of safety in a situation that was unsafe, of control in a situation that was terrifyingly unpredictable, of power in a situation of helplessness.

I struggled to find my place in this world. "What is the meaning to my life?" I often wondered. I was trapped in an abusive environment and faced with the frightening task of adapting to the impossible. Home was a constant fight. School was a constant fight. Life was a constant fight.

My time at Pine Rest didn't cure anything; I was rebellious as ever. There is a sense of power in being stubbornly uncorrectable. I became a belligerent child.

Mother tried to get outside help again, by sending me to a Christian counselor who had a mall ministry. His name is Ken Navis. I bucked it back then but today, I have to give her credit for seeking outside help. She must've realized she was helpless on her own.

The counselor was a nice, gentle soul, and I had a few sessions with him, but I didn't want to listen to him. He told me that I was forgiven and that Jesus died for me. It was the same thing I heard in church and catechism classes. It meant nothing to me.

In the meantime, I was being bullied, ridiculed and attacked in school on a daily basis. Kids can be so cruel. I had such a bad case of acne in junior high and high school that I tried to cover by wearing long bangs. Kids lurked around corners and when I walked by, they jumped me, held me down, and threw my bangs back, saying, "UEEE, look at her pimples." School was not a safe place for me.

I'm the baby of six. I was constantly being picked on by my older siblings. My parents knew I was being kicked around but they ignored it. No one at home ever inquired about my day. My parents never once reviewed my report card, never once attended a parent-teacher conference, and never once watched any sporting events I played in.

Dad used to beat me and my sister Betty so badly that we went to school with welts on our backs, legs, and arms. We had to take our shirts off, bend over and put our hands on the bed, when he gave us the belt, while we screamed in pain with every whip. We were whipped for coming home after curfew, or for talking back and many times for no reason at all.

One day, when we were eleven and twelve years old, Dad beat my brother Ken so bad that my mother hollered at him to stop. Ken was sixteen years old. Mom said, "You better knock it off. You're going to kill him." But it continued. Dad threw Ken down the steps. Ken was vomiting all the way down and Dad kicked him after he got to the bottom. Betty and I held onto each other in fear as we watched, helplessly. Ken had been drinking and came home after curfew.

Total dysfunction and lots of violence was the norm for us. It's how we rolled. It was only logical to us to fight violence with violence. When Betty was beaten to a pulp by her boyfriend at age sixteen, Ken vowed to get him. He hunted down Betty's boyfriend but ended up only threatening him.

My parents' response to our "bad behavior" was: "Now stop that! What would the neighbors think?"

We attended a Dutch denomination church every Sunday. I thought there were a lot of rules in the church. I came to see the church as very strict; I feared them. There was a strong culture of shame. Not talking about anything or you'd be judged was understood; self-expression was taboo. To me, it seemed their image was more of a priority to them than bringing others to God. I saw them as hypocrites who wanted to keep secrets hidden under a sugar coating.

———•———

I hated school. I hated home. I hated life. I hated me. I never stood up for myself, both because I didn't know how, and because I didn't think I was worth it. After all, no one else ever stood up for me or fought to protect me, so why would I fight for me? I learned to hang my head in shame and to never speak up. I came to believe I had it coming. The unaddressed traumas in my life had taught me to be a victim. That I could be a victor in anything never occurred to me.

———•———

After I got out of Pine Rest, I eventually wrote letters to my brothers in Vietnam and told them how much I hated school and life. I'm not sure why I decided to write them, because they picked on me a lot, too. I didn't mention the rapes. I was too ashamed.

I told them about the bullying in school in these letters and it felt good to write down all my feelings. To my surprise, Ken responded with encouraging letters. I read them over and over again. I have one almost memorized. It began, "Ruth, I am over here playing the serious game of war." It continued, "You have to hold your head up high at school, Ruth. You are one of us and there is no reason to hang your head in shame." No one had ever said that to me before. Oh how I wished my brothers were home.

Given how much my mother and oldest sister Bonnie cried when the boys were in Vietnam; it felt like we'd already seen the last of them. They were my last hope. I was really on my own now.

I never went to prom. I went to football games but not to watch the game. I never graduated from high school. I was in constant pursuit of love and safety—but looking for them in all the wrong places.

As a teen, I ran away from home to be with dad. I boarded a Greyhound bus and had to travel five hours. *Maybe I could find solace there, with Dad and his new girlfriend.* (Maybe she was his wife by now, I can't remember.)

I don't understand how children were allowed to travel alone like that. I don't remember purchasing the ticket. Maybe Mom got it for me, I'm not sure.

I hated it when my dad's wife told me to call her "Mom." I didn't know her at all. She seemed okay, but it was too soon to trust her, so when she asked me that, I shut her out.

While I was there, Dad took me fishing. I wasn't too crazy about going fishing but it was a way to be with my dad, so I went along with it. He woke me up at five in the morning. We slowly rowed out onto the lake, the thick fog making it difficult to see anything. I quickly lost my sense of direction.

Dad stopped the boat and we anchored—or so I assumed. The fog made it difficult to tell whether we were anchored or drifting. After sitting quietly for a bit with our poles in the water, I noticed Dad was sleeping. I tried to wake him but he wouldn't wake up. I didn't know he had been drinking all night.

I became frightened. I didn't know where we were. I didn't know what to do. All I knew was that Canada was on one side of the lake and my dad's cottage was somewhere close by. Then, suddenly, the boat crashed into something. To my surprise, it was the dock in front of his cottage.

It's kind of funny now, but at the time I was so relieved that we weren't drifting aimlessly into the lake. The reality of how unreliable my dad was, however, wasn't so funny.

Even after all the beatings I'd taken from him, I believed he was a superhero for a long time, but my fantasy of my dad as my hero started to wither that day. I tried one more time to run away from Mom to be with him, but he was drunk that time, too, so I eventually lost interest in escaping my regular life to be with him. I accepted that Dad just wasn't an option anymore.

He died from a heart attack and alcoholism at age sixty when I was twenty-six and lost in "the life." I wish I could have known him when I was drug free, and when he was sober.

CHAPTER FIVE

I Get "Turned Out"

That same year, (I must have been 14 or 15 years old) my neighborhood friend, Thelma and I knew some hippies who had an apartment near downtown. It was a big party house, with everyone in the building getting high together. They drank and smoked marijuana. I tried both and I didn't like either one.

There was a guy named Pete who lived alone and had a beautiful malamute husky dog named Spanky. Pete loved that dog; they were together all the time unless he was at work.

One day, Pete asked me to look after Spanky while he worked. Spanky had to be tied up all day or in the apartment, but he couldn't be alone in the apartment, so Pete offered his apartment to me if I looked after his dog. I obliged, simply because having his apartment gave me an out from having to go back home.

After Pete left and I was left alone with Spanky, the dog changed: his hair stood up on his back as he showed me his teeth. I screamed for the neighbor lady to come help me and she did. I was able to get away from Spanky, but not without a bite on my wrist.

It was deep and bleeding a lot, so I went to the emergency room to be treated for it.

While in the waiting room, Thelma and I met two black men who seemed really cool: Charles and Richard. They were seated on the other side of the room with women we assumed were their wives. They gave us the eye when their women weren't looking. We giggled and smiled back at them. We were just kids, and boy crazy.

In my opinion, "boy crazy" is a term that is used to make the vulnerabilities of young girls seem cute. Knowing how predators work should make us all see that being boy crazy at age fifteen is not cute at all. It's dangerous. Today I hope parents teach their daughters how to recognize the dangers of being boy crazy.

The men made their move after their women were led out by a nurse. They flirted with us and told us how pretty we were. I was so desperate for positive attention that I was easily reeled in by their compliments and totally impressed with their nice clothes and jewelry.

A nurse who was sitting behind the nurse's station was watching us and when I made eye contact with her she glared at me. If looks could kill, I would've been dead. It was obvious to me that she was irritated by us and by what was going on in the waiting room. I hoped she was not going to be the one to call me in, but she was. She had whispered something to another nurse about us and I assumed they were conspiring against me. I was reluctant to follow her to the room where the doctor was waiting, but I had no choice. I didn't dare speak up. I figured she was just jealous of me, but nonetheless, at that age I still felt intimidated by her. She was supposed to be there to help me; not shoot hate darts at me with her eyes.

The doctor was a nice man. He pulled up a stool, sat down and faced me after I was seated. He examined the dog bites and explained the procedures to me. The nurse stood behind him with her arms folded and with a stern look on her face while the doctor talked to me. I didn't feel comfortable with her in the room but, again, I had no choice. They were in control, not me.

When I was released, they weren't concerned about who I was being released to, either. Two 15-year-old girls walking away from an E.R. visit, on foot, without an adult should have been a red flag to them. They didn't ask any questions about how I got bit by a dog, or where, or who I was with. All their questions were geared towards my treatment and that's it. At that point, I think I would have answered questions about my life if they had asked me. Granted, the experience I had with medical professionals at the hospital when I was thirteen made me leery of them, but I hadn't yet developed the belief that they were all bad. This hospital visit was a lost opportunity.

Thelma and I left and saw Charles and Richard in the parking lot getting into a big, fancy car with the two women. It was exciting. To us, they were so debonair. I hoped they would call soon.

They did. Thelma and I saw those guys regularly. They paid a lot of attention to us. They took us down to the strip and we "were allowed" to come along to the gambling houses they frequented. We became part of "the scene."

Charles drove us around in his fancy car. I soon learned that the gambling houses were also drug houses. That was exciting to us, too. To be trusted with the secrets of the "underground" made me feel special. He appeared to be a smooth businessman, and everyone seemed to respect him wherever we went. I assumed he was committing crimes of some kind, but he would often remind me that he was in control and not to worry because he wouldn't let anything happen to me. He said the less I knew the better, that he would protect me and keep me out of danger. I felt safe with him. When were pulled over by the police Charles always knew what to say and how to handle it. I was impressed by this, too. He reminded me often that he was smarter than the police.

When I look back at this, it saddens me that a child would feel safe with a predator and see the police as the bad guys.

Then Charles introduced me to a woman who would help me pick out some new clothes.

"Yippee! We're going shopping! This is it!" It was so cool. They bought me a hot pants outfit and told me I looked absolutely stunning in my new clothes. I heard them argue about what clothes and accessories I should wear. Wow! They were fighting over me. It felt good. I was drawn in. My hero has arrived!!! I didn't realize they were grooming me for the strip.

I took my new clothes home. My parents were back together again and they were in the basement, playing cards with another couple. I went to the bedroom, changed into the hot pants, and headed for the door. My "boyfriend" Charles was waiting for me in the driveway in his gold Cadillac. Before I could leave, Mother came up from the basement and saw me. She looked out the door and saw Charles waiting for me. She gave me a look of disgust and said, "Hurry up, get out of here. Don't let anyone see you dressed like a slut. What would the neighbors think?"

Dressed like a slut? I didn't think so. Little did she know I didn't have a say in choosing these clothes. Someone else picked them out. How could she expect me to see it her way when she never sat me down and taught me anything? Charles was the first one who ever took the time to advise me what clothes were "appropriate" to wear. She never taught me how to dress, so how could she feel justified in knocking me for the way I dressed? Plus, she could clearly see she didn't buy these clothes for me, but she let it go.

She let ME go in spite of all the red flags of danger!

Charles told me that he had run out of money. I could tell by the look on his face that it was hard for him to tell me that we weren't going to be able to keep going to the places we wanted to go to anymore. Of course, I know now it was all an act on his part. He said he had lost a lot of money at that gambling house. My heart went out to him as he explained that he didn't even have any money for gas in his car to pick me up anymore. I was devastated at the thought of losing my hero. I believed he was just as afraid of losing me as I was of losing him.

He offered me some hope though. He said he knew of a way "we" could get back the money he had lost and we could still do all the things we like to do together. I didn't understand what he meant, but if there was any way I could keep our happy life from ending, I was all for it.

I see now that he knew he had me right where he wanted me. He took me down to the strip, and showed off the new "stunning look" of my "makeover." I was so proud because I knew I was looking good and I had my man by my side. I was so proud to hear Charles brag about me to others.

(My heart goes out to this little girl. I was so naïve.)

I was enjoying how the girls on the street envied me and the pimps were after me. Charles told everybody I was his queen. I was on cloud nine.

I don't remember having a conversation with him about the prior rapes, but I'm sure I told him. I told him all of my problems. He told me I was stupid for allowing those men to have me for free. I was confused and embarrassed that I had done something that he deemed as stupid. All this added to my shame and he knew it.

I thought about how my parents, the hospital, and the police blamed and shamed me for what the rapists did to me. I came to believe that I really *was* stupid and that I really *did* "let them have me." I was convinced I could shed this shame by getting paid to do it now. I figured THIS is why my mother called me a whore. THIS is why my father beat me, and THIS is why the police and healthcare workers walked on out me; *because I'm so stupid.* I didn't want to be stupid anymore.

The self-blaming attitude I acquired from the rapes was re-inforced when Charles told me I was stupid. This kept me from putting any fault on him for anything. I later learned this is called Stockholm syndrome, a psychological phenomenon in which hostages express empathy and sympathy toward their captors, sometimes to the point of defending and identifying with them and coming to be dependent on them.

In my day, there were players' clubs and conventions where these psychopaths gathered together to exchange the brainwashing techniques that had proven successful for them. Now there are books available online that teach these same brainwashing techniques to ensure that pimps can get their prey to accepting an attitude of servitude and keep them submissive. These books teach how to commit a crime! To me, they should be illegal.

Charles took me to one of the gambling houses and I was led to the bedroom where I would earn the money. I didn't realize at the time that this was probably a house where sex trafficking deals were carried out on a daily basis; I thought I was the first one to do this there.

Then I saw the four men.

I was confused at first, not real sure what I was in for, but when the reality of what was about to happen slapped me in the face, I was struck with sheer terror. Fear ripped through me like a knife. I wanted to scream and cry for help, but I didn't dare. They were so much bigger than me and so much more powerful. I was thrown onto the bed and they all approached me at once, with smiles on their faces. I was terrified. No child could assume they had a chance in this situation. I wanted to run but I was afraid of what they would do if I did. I'm sure it was obvious to them how scared I was, but they weren't moved by it.

I thought of what my boyfriend told me about how he felt about women who didn't keep their word and I didn't think I could change my mind.

I was just a child and they were adults. It was a gang rape!

Charles said he was proud of me and took me in his arms. At the time I didn't see being in his arms as twisted and backwards. All I knew was that I was in his arms and that it was over and I felt safe again. I cried and cried in his chest as he apologized for the pain I endured; he thanked me at the same time.

(This part is still very hard for me to revisit today without crying.)

I know now that I was confusing his approval with love and safety—just like he wanted me to. Only a psychopath could find it in himself to do this to a child.

I was only fifteen and already a victim when I met Charles. But, I was not a whore. I was not sexually depraved. I was just a confused little girl. Neither children nor adults can be willing participants in their own abuse.

———•———

After I escaped the life and in the beginning stages of my recovery, I blamed my mother for years for letting me get in Charles' car that night. She had to have known what was likely going on. She let me go off with an older man she never even met. She never inquired or asked questions; she just let me go. She was too worried about what the neighbors would think.

When victims finally identify themselves as victims they have a lot of anger to sort through. The beginning stages of recovery can take a long time simply because there is so much built up anger that has to be unloaded.

Today, after hearing from other survivors that their mothers looked the other way, too, I can truly see the need for all parents to take child protection training classes. They are available now. Child Advocacy Centers say children need to learn about sex from their parents before age nine. This makes so much sense to me. (See websites and resource page).

Through therapy I learned that when we are threatened with danger, our bodies summon a tremendous amount of energy to fight, flee, or freeze, which explained why I froze during the rapes. When faced with the inability to escape, this energy short circuits. These short circuits ricochet through a person's body and mind while the violence is happening, which can result in shock, dissociation, and other kinds of involuntary responses. This short circuit stays with us long after the violence ends, and can live on in the mind, body and spirit in a variety of ways.

Pimps who use force are called *gorilla pimps*. You don't have to be confused or an abused person to fall prey to gorilla pimps. Just walking alone in a dark parking lot can make you vulnerable to gorilla pimps. They use force, kidnapping and/or date rape drugs to nab their victims. Just accepting bottled water that was tainted with drugs can make you fall prey to them.

After they nab their victims it is common for them to take pictures of the victim being raped. They then threaten to show the pictures to the victims' families, churches or employers, and to put them on social media. When the victims learn they were gang raped for money while unconscious from the drug, they are told they would be arrested for prostitution if the police saw the pictures. Traffickers inflict so much shame onto their victims that they are too scared to come forward.

I was drawn into the sex trade by a *Romeo pimp*. I had come to associate sex with affection, love, and safety just like Charles wanted me to. He didn't participate in the gang rape. Even after time went on, he was never sexual with me. I wondered why. Did he not want me? Did I do something wrong?

Now that I look back, I'm sure Charles withheld affection from me as a strategy of some kind that he learned at a players' convention. Whatever the reason, my relationship with Charles was short. I said "relationship" because that's how I thought of it. Pimps are not called pimps by women in the sex trade; they are called boyfriends, husbands, and friends.

———•———

I learned quickly that pimps compete for 'their women.' If a pimp fails at breaking a woman's loyalty to her present "boyfriend" with his flattery and promises, he tries force.

Lewis was one pimp who promised me the world, but he couldn't break my loyalty to Charles with just his charm. He said he would take so much better care of me than Charles. He said, "Baby you just don't understand your potential. You are a gold mine!! I can take you places that Charles can't take you."

He showed up at my house one night. I went outside and jumped in his car, but told him my mom wouldn't let me leave. He became insistent, "Get your coat, Ruth, and let's go!"

I went back inside and told Mother, once again, that he wanted me to leave with him. She told me to get rid of him. I was hoping she would go out there and do it for me, but she didn't. I went back outside, jumped in his car, and said, "Lewis, I can't go."

To my astonishment, he threw the car into drive and stepped on the gas. He parked behind a house somewhere near the strip and got out of the car to pop the hood. When he hooked the battery cables to the battery, I became suspicious. I remembered hearing from others in the street that pimps whipped 'their women' with battery cables. Hearing this didn't scare me at first though, because I figured only women who misbehaved were whipped; I had no intentions of misbehaving. Plus, Charles would never do that to me because he said, 'I was the girl he had always been looking for'.

But Lewis wanted to be a pimp real bad. He ordered me out of the car and I got out. When I saw my chance, I ran. I headed for the strip to find my "comrades."

I didn't find anyone I knew hanging out, so I stood on a corner. I was so afraid Lewis would pull up. I couldn't call the police because I figured they knew me from being with those guys and they'd probably arrest me, thinking I was a common prostitute. My past experience with the police at the hospital made me fear them. So its understandable that I felt relieved when Charles told me he would protect me from them.

I prayed for a kind john to pull up, or even another pimp who would be glad to "rescue me" from Lewis. I ended up getting in a car with a john who was old enough to be my grandfather. He wanted sex, but he wasn't demanding, thank God, and he gave me a ride home.

Mother never asked what happened. Maybe she never even noticed that I had left with him.

———•———

Later, I heard Lewis proudly tell others that he was the one who "turned me out," which means beat me or groomed me to the point of submission and/or acceptance. I didn't understand this term at the time but it didn't take long to catch on.

I was so young. How can anyone just ride by a scared, young girl who is standing on the corner in the dark and not help her? How can a police officer see her as a criminal?

I did a lot of research to get the timeline straight on my life but I wasn't able to retrieve any records from back in the 60s. I was told these records were destroyed, so I have to depend on my memory on the incidents with police when I was a teen.

———•———

I was arrested several times as a child for prostitution and runaway. I can remember these events only in images but I clearly remember the helplessness and fear.

Once, I was in the back seat of a cop car on my way to the juvenile home, crying and crying. The two police officers in the front were scolding me about running away. They told me I was in trouble again because I committed a crime. I noticed the back door was unlocked and when we went over the expressway I tried to jump out. Before I jumped I said, "My dad wouldn't let you do this to me!" The officer in the passenger seat was able to catch me and he held on to my arm the rest of the trip to ensure I wouldn't jump again. They were both silent the rest of the way, as I cried to them about how much I hated them and that I wanted my dad.

I think this happened after I returned from running away from Mom to Dad's house. Today's police cars are better equipped to keep anyone from jumping out of the back seat. They also have cage wire between the front and back seats.

The police saw me as one of the bad guys. How could I believe anything different?

After I was arrested for prostitution, both Mom and Dad came to the juvenile home to visit me. The visiting area was in a room with open space and no restrictions. We sat at a table and I talked about what my cell was like. I don't remember much about the conversation, but when mother asked me about how the food was, I told her, "We are having chicken tonight and it's so good." She slammed her fist on the table and said, "Ok, well if you like it here so much, you can just stay here." Slamming her fist on the table got the attention of the staff and Mom and Dad had to leave. I had to accept it, once again that I was on my own and that there was no way that I was going to get out of there anytime soon and go home.

I think mother was desperate for someone to appreciate her, and this desperation kept her from being able to mother her kids. She looked to us to fulfill her needs and we looked to her to fulfill our needs. Dad wasn't able to focus on our needs, either. He had too many of his own needs, fighting his own demons, after being in war. He was in World War II. I know he suffered from PTSD. It was called shell shock back then.

CHAPTER SIX

Sex And Violence Are My "Normal"

I was sent to an alternative school when I was sixteen—a school for 'unruly' kids.

The teachers and students were mostly black; I think there were only three other white kids. Today, mixing black and white students is commonplace, but back then it was new.

I really liked my teacher. He was nice. I wanted to be teacher's favorite. One day, he gave me a ride to a friend's apartment in the same neighborhood as the alternative school. He came inside and it was just me and him; no one else was home. Once again, I felt powerless. In my mind I had to comply if I wanted to be teacher's favorite.

He raped me and then told me he wanted to keep "our relationship" going, but it had to be a secret. I didn't resist him. I thought I was going to be treated real special by pleasing him. Oh, how I wanted to feel special. I agreed to keep it a secret.

Even though I cooperated with him, I still call it rape because I was just a child and he was my adult teacher. He played on my naivety and took advantage of my vulnerabilities. How could I accuse an upstanding teacher of a crime, even if I did see it as a crime? No one would believe me, a runaway and drop out, anyway. I really was powerless. Back then, this kind of thing was unheard of. Talking about it was breaking an unspoken rule.

The other students could sense I was teacher's favorite, and some black, female students planned to "get me." One day, while I was waiting for the elevator by the stairway, they jumped me, punching and kicking me. I managed to break free from them and ran down the steps to get out.

Where was my teacher? I expected him to defend me. No one did. No one stopped me from leaving after the fight broke up. I was on my own with that one, too. None of the teachers or authorities at this school ever addressed the incident. I never went back to school after that.

Teachers and parents need to be aware of children who display jealousy towards other students. It's common for teens to compete with each other for a teacher's attention and very possibly inappropriate affection. I deemed inappropriate affection as a normal way of showing that I was special and teacher's favorite.

———•———

I guess you could say I moved out of the house at age sixteen. I crashed at different places, hopping around with "friends" for years.

By the time I was seventeen, I had a lengthy police record and I was a high school dropout. I knew my family wasn't proud of me. How could I be proud of myself?

By the time I was twenty, I had burned bridges with family and friends. I didn't think I could ever land a regular job. Who would I put down on a job application as a reference? I believed there was no hope for me.

I couldn't even fathom leading a respectable life. I didn't know what self-respect was. I accepted my fate: that quenching men's sexual desires was all I was good for.

At age sixteen, I guess I had finally given up on my hero ever showing up. In order to endure that way of life, I had to become numb to my feelings. I had to do what my counselor calls "dissociate," which means "disconnect" or "think of something else so you're not focusing on the pain."

Drugs helped me to dissociate. A pimp taught me how to use heroin when I was sixteen. Before I started using it, I was instructed not to interrupt anyone that was in a "nod" from a heroin high because that can ruin the high, so when I saw the pimps and girls "nodding," I tiptoed around them.

It seemed so strange to me. How could anyone enjoy sleeping in a chair with their chin on their chest? *You call that fun?* But the first time I tried it, I fell in love with it and I understood. The high altered my reality. Shame was my life, but drugs helped me live with it, helped me deny it, and helped me bury it. Plus, I was in the in-crowd now, and I felt accepted.

It didn't take long before I was hooked on drugs, and having to support that habit kept me taking crap from johns, pimps, and cops: I had to keep working.

As long as I was high, all the crap was okay with me, but because abusing drugs keep you from maturing emotionally and spiritually, my confusion and shame continued. Being addicted left me open to the continued abuse and victimization by my traffickers. I believed I was the scum of the earth. Sometimes I thought about God, and what others had told me about Him, but it all sounded so mysterious and remote. I got advice from people and family, but they had no idea what I needed or what I was suffering from. I wouldn't listen to anyone anyway. Their solutions were too simple for my huge issues so I blocked them out. To me, there was no such thing as God—not one who was on my side anyway. What I knew for sure was that there was no way out for me. Even though I was focused on survival, I really didn't care if I lived or died.

My siblings and I parted ways when I was in my teens. They were starting their own lives and families, and we never heard from each other except for maybe holidays, when I was in jail, or when we ran into each other at Mother's house. At thirteen and fourteen years old I felt confused and surprised when they moved on to raise children of their own. I was a child, too! I guess that's why I expected parenting from them when my parents failed me so badly.

At age 18, I'm an adult and I'm suddenly supposed to have life figured out and know what went wrong? I was just as confused during my childhood as in my adulthood after being so badly abused but I WAS expected by society, law enforcement and others to have life figured out by now.

When every adult in a child's life fails them, including family, church, law enforcement and healthcare professionals, strategies for survival are honed. Without intervention they carry their untold stories into adulthood, which even they themselves can't put into words or make sense of. Continually being misunderstood keeps victims in survival mode and from self-identifying as victims. They need you to hear what they are NOT saying. Help them tell their stories so healing can begin.

I got a ride to Mom's house one day when I was about nineteen, only to find the house empty: she had moved in with her new husband. Wow! Mom had another priority in her life. What could I do? I felt so lost, but I had to put it behind me. I had to figure out what was next.

Back then, it wasn't difficult to get rent vouchers from the government. My friend Thelma and I shared apartments for about three years while we were on welfare, but when she got pregnant, we parted ways. I don't know what became of her after that.

In the beginning of being trafficked, several pimps exploited me. They would come and go just like the johns did—just like everyone in my life did. I didn't believe I had control of who was allowed in my life. I was beaten, threatened with guns, and thrown out of cars and into jails. It was a life of overwhelming loneliness; I lived in fear and desperation every day. Nothing was my own, not my belongings and not my body. Pimps would hit me and shout, "You're going to learn to appreciate what I've done for you, if I have to beat it in you!"

Nothing made sense; it was all crazy and chaotic. I came to believe I could avoid beatings and gain approval if I produced or performed well.

My relationship with Charles was short. Charles told me he wanted to take me to New York and I'd be his queen. I think he ended up going to New York without me simply because he couldn't find me when it was time for him to leave the area. I thank God for that.

From ages 20 to 27, I was fiercely loyal to Mark until he went to prison. After Mark was gone, I met Carlos and was with him until age 33. Both Mark and Carlos kept me under their control by isolating me from outside support and resources.

Traffickers teach their victims that anyone who's not in "the game" is a square and can't be trusted. When victims fall for this, they become isolated from anyone who could help them. I fell for it. I learned to trust no one but them. I told others they were my boyfriends.

Mark constantly threatened to beat me. Just looking at the driver in the car beside us at a red light meant I'd get punched. One day he beat me so badly that he had to take me to the hospital. After seeing the cuts and bruises on my face, he told me, "I'll make your face so scarred up that every time you look in the mirror, you will think of me."

We arrived at the hospital and he went in with me. I don't

remember a lot about this E.R. visit, but I do know he was told to wait in the waiting room and he didn't like that. He wanted to be with me throughout the whole visit to make sure I didn't ask anyone to help me and that I didn't expose him. While alone with the medical staff, I had the chance to talk freely with them and I could have told them everything, but I just didn't dare. I figured they wouldn't help me, that they were there because they had to be. They had a job to do and, after all, why would anyone help me? Plus, they had other patients they had to get to.

After I was treated, Mark was allowed to come in to see me. Both of my eyes were swollen shut. I couldn't see him but I knew he was there when he held my hand. I cried and cried to him, asking him, "Why?" I pleaded with him and told him I thought he loved me and I couldn't understand why.

He bent over to whisper in my ear. "You better quit talking so damn loud. These m___f____s here don't need to know all of our damn business. Now shut up!"

Obviously, the staff was nearby and I'm sure they heard everything I said, but I guess they didn't want to get involved. Not getting involved was just the culture; couples needed to work out their own problems.

That beating inflicted enough fear in me to make me always aware of my behavior and my words when I was with him, and even when I wasn't.

Everybody assumed I chose that life, and because of that assumption, I was shunned. Everyone treated me as fallen, as incapable of speaking for myself; even if I did speak, they discounted what I said. I was an invisible member of society.

The strong "slut-shaming" culture against the women who fall prey to sex traffickers kept me in my place. The stigma left me with no one to turn to. It's obvious to me now that I wasn't safe with Mark or Carlos, but I was safer with them than anywhere else.

How can that be true? My abusers were the only ones I had. In order to protect their income or in order to support their drug habit, they had to indirectly protect me. This was the only protection that was offered to me by anyone, anywhere, so I valued the little they offered. They were also my connection to drugs.

I was navigating through my adult life with the victim mindset, and I'm sure it was obvious how little I thought of myself. It was definitely obvious to those who took advantage of me and my confusion.

The victim mindset blinded me from seeing what was right in front of me. When people reached out to me, they were faced with my fierce rebellion—I defended my traffickers for a very long time, insisting on calling them my boyfriends and having them over to family Christmas parties.

Now I can clearly see that protecting my wellbeing was the last thing on my traffickers' minds. I supplied us with everything to keep our relationship intact. It was all at my expense while they reaped the benefits. Drugs were the only benefit in it for me.

Life is not compassionate to those with a victim mindset. We need to empower our children so they will know how to protect themselves.

I was constantly in survival mode. I was a victim but I didn't identify as a victim. I didn't recognize how I had been victimized. I thought I was just a whore who had it coming. I sabotaged positive relationships and any offers of help. I developed severe trust issues. Those with a victim mindset aren't compassionate to even themselves.

Many people keep working for demeaning bosses for fear of being financially destitute. Many avoid jumping out of airplanes for fear of dying. Many don't voice their opinion for fear of being rejected. A trafficked woman stays with her trafficker because of all three.

Mark had another girl. I didn't know it for a long time. I wanted to be his only one but I had to accept that I wasn't. Even after all the beatings, I always thought he would change and it would get better. He introduced me to her one day and explained that she was a good "booster," a good shoplifter. He told me she had a trunk load of brand new clothes that we could get cash refunds for. They taught me how to talk clerks into giving me a cash refund without a receipt.

I didn't look like the street type, nor did I look like a drug addict. Until I was around thirty, I looked like the girl next door. I didn't dress provocatively nor did I portray a bad-ass attitude. My innocent look was advantageous for Mark. He told me I was the only one who would be believed, so I was the one who had to go into the store with the stolen clothing.

My heart raced as I walked through the store. I tried hard not to let my fear show to the clerk. Mark reminded me of the beatings I'd already taken from him, and I didn't want that to happen again. I came back out of the store with the money and fended off his rage and we headed for the dope house for my reward.

I did this for a while until the other girl got caught stealing; then I was taught how to boost. I was so afraid while in the store. I saw security walking around, but I couldn't come out until I had the most expensive items with me. The very first time I walked out with an arm full of clothes I was followed by security and arrested.

When you function on a daily basis with fear in the back of your mind, you are blinded from seeing what is right in front you. I knew stealing was wrong, but I was focused on avoiding beatings and getting drugs.

Carlos was a drug-dealing and drug-using pimp. He lured me into a volatile relationship with him by giving me free drugs, but he got more and more demanding and expected more and more money from me. Drug dealers easily lose their trusted drug connections if they use the drugs they are selling. His addiction got out of hand and he got over his head in debt with his connections. He eventually was on the run from them, which meant I was over my head in debt with him, because he expected me to get him out of this debt.

He had other girls working for him when I first met him. I didn't want anything to do with that; I just wanted to score drugs. Many feared him, including me. Carlos was a real psychopath.

He locked me up in an apartment with him once, while he held me at gunpoint and did drugs for two days. I wondered whether I would make out of there alive. He was taking large amounts of drugs and his behavior got more and more erratic. He ranted on and on about nothing, waving the gun, as he paced back and forth. I didn't dare move.

This maniac held me hostage for two days without sleep or food. I spent so many years trying to please him. I eventually tried to "run away" from him but there was no hiding from him. Other people on the streets would tell him where to find me.

What a mess I was back then! I defended and took care of this man for years! I stayed with him until he was arrested for selling heroin; I was 32 years old. By then, I was able to elude being pimped, but I felt like I was buried alive in a deep hole that I'd never be able to get out of. There was no way out for me, so I relied on what I knew to do.

During my late twenties, after Mom's second husband died, I'd sometimes go to her house, totally exhausted, if I could find a ride. I'd sneak into the garage to sleep in her car, or on her front porch. I'd be gone before she woke up.

No one could understand what I was going through, which left me with the burden of having to prove myself. I tried to prove myself to my parents, my adult siblings, to law enforcement, and then to society in general, to no avail.

I navigated through life by running to and from danger. I escaped a would-be rapist/murderer once by jumping into the passenger seat of a garbage truck while the driver was picking up a trash bin. I could very well have run into even more danger by jumping into that truck, but thank God the driver was a good person, and took me where I asked him to: back to the strip where Carlos was waiting for me.

I still didn't have any money, and both Carlos and I still needed a fix, so I got back to work. Carlos and I chalked up the danger that I had just escaped as just another bad date, a consequence of the trade.

On another "bad date," a potential rapist/murderer had me by the hair, on my knees, along the side of a dirt road on the outskirts of a wooded area. As I begged him not to hurt me, a car with two couples approached, and their headlights shone right on us. The man let go of me and ran into the woods. I threw myself in front of the car to make them stop, crying and screaming. There was no guarantee that they were going to stop but I had to do something. Thank God they stopped; they were good people. The driver parked the car and ran into the woods to catch my assailant, but he had to give up. They tried to convince me that I needed to go to the police station with them, but I did not want the police involved. The bad cops were part of "the game" and I knew that even a seemingly good cop could turn bad when presented with this kind of vulnerability.

There was a period of time when I eluded arrest and it seemed to me it was because of a deal I made with a police officer who patrolled the strip. Because I made myself available to him whenever he asked, other officers didn't bother me. Whenever he picked me up from the strip, though, I was so afraid that someone would see me get into his patrol car, and that would be evidence enough for them to believe that I was snitching.

Carlos never knew about the deal I had with this police officer. He was confident I wouldn't make any deals with the police and his confidence shielded me from being labeled a snitch—which reinforced my dependence on him. As long as the people on the street saw there was someone who was "working with me," they figured I must not be a snitch. Mark and Carlos shielded my street reputation.

On the street, known snitches are hunted down and destroyed. For a long time, the word on the street was that I was working for the police. This protected me a bit, however, because many kept their distance from me for fear of being taped or set-up. But it also made it difficult to score drugs. Many times I had to rely on others to score for me. If Carlos scored for me, I got cheated out of my share, so I tried on my own, to no avail. The chances of being cheated out of drugs by anyone who scored for me was great. Finding a reliable partner on the streets was almost impossible. Living on the streets consisted of taking huge risks.

It's ironic that the harassment by the other officers started up again as soon as the officer I made the deal with was promoted.

There was a period of time when the police were putting the girls in the back seat of unmarked police cars but instead of taking them to jail, they took them miles away from the strip, to a densely wooded area and told them to get out of the car. They said, "Since you like to walk so much, you can walk from here." They left the girls there to find their own way back in the middle of the night. This never happened to me, but I was warned by other girls that it had happened to them.

Trafficked women are very aware of the potential danger that awaits them around every corner. They have to be on constant alert and never let their guard down.

That's how life was.

By the time I was 17 I was under the complete control of my trafficker. I was drug addicted, had a lengthy police record and I was a high school dropout. I knew my family wasn't proud of me. How could I be proud of myself?

CHAPTER SEVEN

Hopes Dashed — Yet Again

Coming close to death is an experience you never forget. One of the most terrifying encounters I had was during the holidays in 1980. Carlos had dropped me off and said he'd be back when I returned to the strip from a date.

There was a snowstorm on New Year's Eve. Carlos and I both needed a fix. I was standing on the corner that night at around 2 a.m., and it was very cold. There was hardly any traffic and I was hoping someone would come along and stop, to at least get me out of the cold.

I got into a car with a man who had put a fifty dollar bill on the passenger seat, in plain sight of anyone who opened the door or looked in the window. I thought maybe he was drunk and didn't realize it was there.

This will be easy money I thought. I jumped in, sat on top of the fifty dollars and he drove behind a factory; but instead of what I was expecting, he pulled out a switchblade (or some sort of sharp weapon). He was aiming for my private parts. He tried slicing me between my legs.

I fought back. I kicked him as hard as I could as I tried to escape. I was able to prevent him from slicing me up but my hands got cuts from defending myself. There were blood stains all over my clothes, coat and on the seat of his car.

Maybe if I yell something in Spanish he will think my pimp had followed us. I reached for the door handle as I frantically fought him off and prayed the door wasn't locked. It wasn't. It opened, and we both fell out of the passenger side door as I screamed, in Spanish, "Carlosl! Ven, ven! Andele, andele!" (Carlos, come, come! Hurry, hurry!)

It worked. The man let me go and took off and I thought I was safe; but then he must have realized I was bluffing, because I saw him turn around and he was coming back to get me.

I had to get out of the road so he couldn't run me over so I ran into a snow-covered, open field. I heard the sound of the engine and it was getting closer and closer. I frantically searched for some kind of hiding spot but couldn't find anything to hide behind. I finally decided to just lie flat in the snow. He didn't see me. He circled the block and came around the field several times and then I heard the sound of the engine diminish.

I took my chances and made another run for it, up a hill but I could hear the engine again; he was coming back. I saw a dumpster nearby so I climbed into it by boosting myself up from a pile of dirt that was on the side of it. I fell into it and thank God it was empty.

Once I was in there, I was afraid I wasn't going to be able to get back out. It was so dark in there. I could hear his engine again as he went around and around the dumpster. He was so close!

After a bit, when I didn't hear his car anymore, I hoisted myself out with the help of a ledge that I felt with my feet. I headed for a nearby house where I knew a dope dealer lived, but when I got to the top of the hill, I heard the car engine again.

This time I ducked under a car that was parked in someone's driveway. The house was filled with people and I heard loud Spanish music as I lay under the car in the freezing temperatures, hoping not to be noticed by the 'john' or the partiers inside.

I heard his engine again and I watched him slowly drive by. He kept on going because he didn't see me under the car. When the sound of his engine diminished again, I made another run for it.

Finally, I made it to the dealer's house and collapsed on his kitchen floor. My coat and clothes had bloody stains all over it. No one there wanted to call the cops and neither did I. There was no one else that I could call. I figured Carlos gave up on waiting for my return and looked for his own way to score. He probably asked the dealer to 'loan' him some dope until his woman returned from a date.

There were no cell phones back then. I used the dealer's phone and called another 'john' named Henry and asked him to pick me up. The thought of staying the night with another 'john' made me sick, but at least I knew his place was safer and I really had no other options. I didn't have any money to pay a pimp for help. I could pay a john though.

Henry poured a solution of hydrogen peroxide and rubbing alcohol into the bathroom sink so I could dip my hands in it to clean them off. The moment my hands came in contact with the solution, I screamed because it burned so bad. He had to forcefully hold my hands in the solution because it was a natural reaction to pull back from the pain.

I called on Henry quite a bit when I needed respite. I always kept a change of clothes at his place. He was a reliable source of "income" and transportation for me for a long time. He did for me as long as I "did for him".

In the streets, 'johns' were considered the scum of the earth by the pimps and their women. They are considered unmanly and 'square.'

Pimps convince their women to lose respect for anyone who is not in 'the game.' This is a way to keep them isolated from anyone who might reach out to them. Pimps sever the victims' ties to outside help and resources. I believed Carlos was the only one on my side.

The next day was our belated family Christmas party, which was held at a school that was being rented as my mother's church. A lot of family was there and I couldn't wait to get to the party. I wanted to be with my family so badly.

I had brought Carlos to our family Christmas parties before, but I had lost track of him when I came across the "bad date" the night before so he didn't go with me to this party. Henry dropped me off there.

For once, I wanted to tell my family what had happened to me. I wanted them to know how scared I was, and I wanted to collapse in someone's arms and be held. I wanted someone to let me cry it out and "make it all better." I was hoping to hear them say that they were so glad I was still alive.

I got the opposite. No one would speak to me; not even Betty. I had looked to her for guidance when we were little, but I could no longer count on her. She played cards with the family and they all ignored me, like I wasn't there. I was so hurt.

I know...I know...I had been stealing from them and lying to them and all, but I was just almost murdered! I felt like that didn't matter to them, either.

I couldn't believe it. Did my family think I wanted this life? Did they think that all that was happening to me was something I knowingly signed up for? Again, my hero never showed up. To me, it seemed like all the heroes in my life were heroes to everyone but me.

I watched my family act so lovingly with each other. I watched them show love to their wives and children and I couldn't help but wonder how they ended up with love in their lives and how did I miss out? I knew they would protect their own kids with their very lives. They would never protect me like that, even though I was their kid sister. I had to face it, they wouldn't protect me like that now either.

I saw life from the position of a victim; the scum of the earth who will never be accepted or fit in anywhere. I reasoned everything to fit this concept.

Now that I'm sixty one, I see it totally differently. At the time, it never dawned on me that my family was just as confused as I was. I expected parenting from my siblings and I'm sure they wondered why I ended up so lost. My family was forced into protection mode of themselves and their families because I had manipulated all of them so many times and they'd had enough of it. They came to expect the worst from me. I had played on their emotions for money, given them guilt trips, and cried to them about emergency after emergency and then begged them to come get me out of jail. They were sick of it.

At the time, I saw them as responsible for my mess. I looked for them to make it up to me somehow. I believed they abandoned me, and not the other way around. All of us were so wrong in our expectations. We were simply not educated on how to recognize the signs of abuse or of HT.

I'm sure if my family would have known that I'd been raped by predators who brainwashed me, they would have stepped up and intervened; but they didn't know what I was going through. There was no recourse for them either. It was Christmastime and they wanted to enjoy a festive family time, and then I showed up, the downer who always spoiled the good times. I had cried "Wolf!" one too many times. They simply couldn't trust me anymore.

It was Mother who wanted all of us together for Christmas, but my siblings weren't too keen on that idea. So I didn't tell anyone about the night before. All during the family Christmas party I waited and hoped for the chance to, but no one paid any attention to me. I even tried dropping heavy hints, like hanging my bloody coat near the bathroom door, but nobody asked about it or commented on it, so I chose not to show anyone the cuts on my hands, either.

When it all became clear to me how blind we all were, I realized all the tragedies and injustices. It was hard for me to accept these realities; but holding on to them held me back too.

Yes, there's a lot of sadness in my story. Yes, there's a lot of tragedy in my story, but I had let it go; I had to let it go in order to move forward.

My whole family experienced a lot of trauma and tragedy. Watching how my siblings moved on, led the way for me to do the same. *If they can do it I can do it.*

At the time, I couldn't see how I was the one who delayed my recovery from this life of self- destruction. How could I? I was garbage. I wanted the shame lifted off me, but I thought this had to come from family, or an outsider.

CHAPTER EIGHT

Can Anybody Hear Me?

nother time I narrowly escaped murder was when I was twenty-eight years old. Even in the terror of this close call, there was a ray of hope.

I thought I was going to score some drugs with two Mexican brothers who'd picked me up while I was hanging around a popular drug house. One of them was a double amputee. There was small talk as we rode down the highway to the dealer's place. When they turned down a dark dirt road, I became frightened. They noticed I was nervous and reassured me that we were getting close to the drug dealer's cabin.

Then they stopped the truck in the middle of an orchard and the double amputee, who was in the back seat, put a box cutter knife to my neck. I froze in fear. I knew my life was over. They took turns on me and I cooperated because I feared for my life.

There were moments when I saw a knife on the seat and not in their hands or at my throat and I thought there might be a way for me to run. I also considered grabbing the knife and using it on one of them, but dismissed that idea since I was up against two. They ordered me to change position because they intended to sodomize me.

Again, I was gripped with sheer terror. I felt my body weaken and I almost collapsed. I cried and begged them not to do it. One of them yelled "Turn around."

I simply could not cooperate any longer. I knew they intended to kill me that night, so I had to do whatever I could to get away.

The keys were in the ignition, and since the driver's door was unlocked, I considered taking the keys and tossing them before running.

Then I thought, *the one with legs will catch me and then we'll all be stuck here.*

As I was turning around in the front seat, I made a split second decision to leave the keys in the ignition and I made a run for it.

I knew the double amputee couldn't run after me, but I feared that his brother was right behind me. I was naked and running as fast as I could.

When I saw their headlights coming right at me, I realized the brother with legs had gotten behind the wheel. He tried to run me over, but I zig-zagged between the trees and he kept missing me. After a while he gave up and I watched the taillights disappear down the dirt road.

I was alone in the apple orchard, naked, cold, and so exhausted. It was very dark. I had no idea where I was, or which way to go. I was so scared, but at the same time, so relieved that they were gone.

After wandering in the dark for maybe an hour, I saw a dot of light in the distance and went towards it. It was the front light of a four-family apartment building. On the way there, I had blindly stepped knee-deep into a creek and fallen in mud. When I finally got there, I was filthy-dirty, but I thanked God for leading me there.

The entrance door in the front was locked. I pounded on the door and a man looked out from his window upstairs. I had no way of covering myself up, and I felt so humiliated. I told him I'd been raped.

He threw me a blanket from the upstairs window and came down the stairs to let me in. I walked up to his apartment with his blanket around me. I was helpless once again. He told me to sit at the kitchen table while he called the police. I was hoping he would call a hero of some kind, not the police. I asked him not to call the police and said I just wanted to call a "friend" of mine, Henry. He took his phone into the living room called the police. He gave me the phone when he was through and I called Henry. I told him what happened and with help from the man in the apartment, I was able to tell him where I was. He said he would bring me some clothes.

There was another man in the apartment too. The place smelled of garbage and there were beer cans and cigarette butts everywhere. I could tell they were both drunk.

Now I'm thinking, *maybe I wandered into even more danger.* While I sat at the kitchen table, I didn't dare move. Neither of the men said anything to me. We just waited.

The police arrived; they recognized me from the street. One cop asked questions and wrote the information down while another cop stared at me. I was filled with rage because I had to sit there which allowed him to just stare at me. I shouted at him, "What the hell you looking at?" I was ready to fight at this point. I was so sick and tired of this mess. I knew they weren't there to help me. It was just a job they had to do.

Henry arrived with my clothes. He had a private conversation with the police while I changed clothes in the man's bathroom. (I wonder what THAT was like.) I was put in the back seat of the police car and we headed for the hospital. Henry met us at the hospital.

I was left alone in the exam room at the hospital for a long enough time that I considered leaving and not going through with the rape kit process. No one consoled me and it was cold in there. I overheard someone say 'I was a common prostitute'. They must have read my police record. It felt like salt had been poured into my open wounds.

A kind detective came into the room. At first, to me he was just another one who had a job to do. I had just a hospital gown on as I laid on the gurney. I couldn't look him in the eye. I felt so ashamed and humiliated. Plus, it was just me and him. He was in control of this situation, not me.

To my surprise, he was so nice. He covered me with a blanket and after getting some information from me he said, "Ruth, I know you didn't ask for this life. You have rights Ruth, and we're gonna get these guys!!"

His words echoed like music to my very soul. No one had ever told me before that they believed I had rights. It sounded to me like this guy was willing to fight for my rights? I was dumbfounded. I had to let that sink in a bit. *If he's going to fight for my rights, I'm ready to fight too.* At this point in my life I was ready to die. I didn't want to go on anymore; it was no use. I was up against the whole world and I just couldn't do it alone anymore. I wondered if he was making empty promises. I wondered that, if truth be told, he really had no intentions on fighting for me. But these words definitely got my attention. I figured I'd better wait to see if his actions were going to back up his words before I trusted him though. But after hearing that there was even a glimmer of hope that these guys would pay for what they did to me, I decided to put my trust in him and in the legal system, for now anyway. I decided to go forward and try to get these guys.

Before the detective left the room, he said, "Before I step out of the room Ruth, is there a trusted person in your life that can come be with you throughout the process tonight?"

I was able to look him in the eye at this point. I didn't feel he was disgusted with me or in a hurry to get on to someone or something else. He was looking beneath the surface. I looked him in the eye and said, "No, there is someone waiting for me in the waiting room with my clothes, but thank you." There was no one in my life I could trust but just being given a choice made me feel more like a human being and more in control.

I thought *he wasn't out to manipulate me for his own benefit, like so many others had, because he asked me if there was someone else **that I trusted**, that he could call for me.* So many others just went through the process and didn't concern themselves with how I might feel in a hospital gown, lying on a gurney, amongst strangers. I thought maybe this guy was a sincere cop after all, but I still needed to see some action.

You see, I had come to believe that the police were not on my side, starting at age 13 years old, when I was interrogated like a criminal. I was expected to perform sexually for some of the arresting police officers too, so why would I call on them? I never knew if I'd encounter a good cop or a bad cop if I called for help. I was afraid to take that chance. Granted, I received perks from the bad cops in exchange for sexual favors before but would you call on them after being raped and sexually assaulted? I had no energy to perform sexually again after being raped.

Plus, to add to the isolation, my traffickers and everyone else on the street reinforced that belief because in the street it was just understood. The fear of being labeled a snitch by those in "the game" and being arrested or abused by the police kept any of us from ever calling the police for help.

I stayed with Henry that night. Calling him was a last resort option though; just like calling the police was. The conditions which Henry helped me in were shallow and narrow. It was understood between us; there was no unconditional, heartfelt concern for each other. I was thankful he had enough sense to let me have my own room.

The next day, I met the detective again at a Burger King. He needed more information. After this meeting I knew I had someone in my corner. He talked like a motivational speaker. He reassured me he would do all he could to get these guys. His motivation was contagious.

I learned that the rapists were from Arizona and were in Michigan staying with family that lived near the popular drug house. I was truthful with the detective. I told him how I thought we were on our way to score some drugs. He stayed in contact with me, even though my life on the street continued.

I went back to the life. I had to. I still had a habit to feed and I knew my boyfriend wouldn't let me go. But I reflected back on what the detective said many times after this. It was like a whisper inside me that kept repeating itself in, "I didn't ask for this life? I have rights?"

Meanwhile, Carlos knew I had another run-in with a bad date but I didn't tell him the whole story. I couldn't let him know I was talking to police. I knew I had to manage this situation on my own again. It became easier to do when Carlos got busted for sales of heroin during the rape investigation.

Now I'm on my own. The word got out that Carlos was in jail. I felt vulnerable and afraid that I would be targeted by those on the street since my "protection" was locked up.

Soon after this meeting with the detective, I saw a car tailgating another very closely while I was hanging around near that popular drug house. I recognized the rapists in the front car, and that the tailgaters were undercover police. Oh Wow!! The rapists were under heavy surveillance! Oh, how this made me feel vindicated! I credited the kind detective who was on the case for this. I didn't trust cops, but this guy was different.

I was approached by a Mexican woman one day, while hanging around that popular drug house. I'd never seen her before in my life.

She said, "Get the cops off my brothers, or you'll be killed." Then she calmly walked away.

Although I had a sinking feeling it wasn't going to turn out well, and I wasn't good at fighting for me, I decided to stick with it, since I had the police to back me up. I put all my trust in the justice system and never changed my story to the cops.

Shortly after the rapists' sister threatened me, I got busted again. The kind detective came to the jail to talk to me; I could tell by the look on his face that he had bad news. The prosecutor had decided not to prosecute!

My heart sank. I felt totally abandoned, all over again. There's nothing like the hopelessness that comes after you've felt a glimmer of hope.

"Why?" I asked.

He said, "The prosecutor felt we didn't have enough evidence to carry through with it."

"Not enough evidence? What do you mean? Does he think I ran through an apple orchard in the middle of the night, naked, just for fun?"

I cried. Oh how I cried! My heart was ripped apart. I was filled with total despair once again. *How many more times will I be kicked to the curb? How many more times will I be so unimportant? How many more people will see me as a waste of time?* **Can anybody hear me?**

The detective said he believed that these guys had done this to other women before, and that they'd do it again. I knew they would too. Their truck was rigged in a way to accommodate the double amputee's position in a sex act. But they remained free.

Once again, they walked out on me!

The detective apologized and left. Once again, I told myself I just wasn't worth fighting for. I was convinced that the reason why the prosecutor wouldn't prosecute was because I was just a common prostitute, and not worth the effort. My past behavior was proof to everyone that I was never going to be any good. Once again, there was no use in going on. I wanted to die.

Even today, I still cry for justice against these men. They could very well be doing this to other women, still. Because of the stigma of prostituted women they are targeted by rapists more than any other. In my day, no one had to fear being prosecuted for raping or sometimes even killing a prostitute.

Today I'm appalled at how some people can believe that anyone could be a willing participant in their own abuse. Abuse is abuse; but many will dance around that fact and they justify their judgmental views by throwing accusations at the victims. They tell themselves, "They asked for it." This keeps THEM from feeling any guilt from their unjustifiable verdicts. This is all twisted and backwards.

I understand that it was the stigma and myths the detective was up against at the police department and prosecutors office. I'm sure the whole police department believed that prostitutes are not capable of being victimized.

The detective didn't win the fight he was in, but I was moved by his kindness to fight for me nonetheless. His kindness made me begin to see the world with a different perspective. I'm sure this experience was an important baby step in my recovery.

CHAPTER NINE

Numb To Everyone And Everything

Human Trafficking has been around for a very long time and because of the studies that have been conducted we now see pimps and traffickers as the psychopaths and child molesters they really are. But then, it was just assumed that prostitutes were in the life by choice. Everyone figured that in this land of the free, we all have freedom of choice, so of course they freely chose that life.

I stopped by mom's house one day when I was twenty-five, deeply lost in the life, needing some reprieve from the street. I walked into the house and said, "Hi," to both Mom and my brother Ken, who was there fixing the roof.

We chatted for a bit, but it was tense. I never got any warm welcomes when my siblings were there. I did my usual thing, got some food out of the fridge and used the bathroom. When I came out of the bathroom Mom and Ken approached me with open arms. I thought it was weird and I felt real uncomfortable.

As they approached me, Ken said, "Ruth we can't do this anymore. We have to let you go."

They both put their arms around me and I tried backing away from them so I could get out of there, but they hugged me even tighter. I couldn't just push them away; after all, this was my mother and brother.

Then Ken started praying.

He cried out, "Dear God, please be with my sister as she goes from here. Guide and protect her, Lord, and show her the way. Help her to be strong and to lean on you."

I was shocked.

When they freed me, Ken said, "You have to go now, and you can't come back."

I left, and in a hurry, too. I didn't know how to take that.

I can't come back? So this is it?

But I quickly put it behind me. I had to "get to work" so I could feed the habit. Plus, I knew Mark would be looking for me soon. I was always aware of how much time I spent away from him, because if too much time went by and he didn't know where I was, I would be in for it when I did see him.

My visits to my mom's weren't really about visiting. I usually came with an underlying motive, when I was in need of something. My family tried and tried with me but had to give up. To them, I was the one to be avoided and feared. They didn't know I had been so victimized, exploited and trafficked. All they knew was that I was a whore and hard-core drug addict, and they expected the worst from me.

I figured I was shunned by my family simply because they didn't love me. To me, they were too busy caring for others who were more worthy of their love.

Once, Ken drove down the strip and saw me standing on a corner. He looked at me as he slowly drove by. I watched his car go off until I couldn't see it anymore. I wanted to read his mind, but with the tough attitude I had developed, I shrugged it off and told myself I didn't care what he was thinking. Neither he nor anyone else could get me off the streets anyway, so I let it go.

Deep down, I was so ashamed. I loved my brother and I knew he loved me. But what could I do? What could he do? I couldn't focus on that or I would cry. I had to keep going. I needed some drugs and a place to stay; I had to "get to work."

Shortly after he was out of my sight, I felt something soft hit my back. I turned around and didn't see anything. But then I got hit again. This time, it hit me on my head. It was eggs: men were throwing eggs at me. My hair and clothes were getting saturated. Then I saw the men in a hotel window. I heard them laugh as they threw the eggs.

I thought of my brother and I lost it. I felt like a little girl in school, being targeted by bullies again. I had to get off the street. I couldn't hold back the tears.

When we were kids, Ken would've "gotten those guys" if he'd known, but now? No way. I wasn't worth defending. It was so profoundly lonely living as an outcast.

I ran down the street to hide. I cried and cried, "Somebody, help me!"

I wasn't the only one suffering from my confusion and addiction. Many times, I was blind to other people's welfare and feelings. Others could be suffering right in front of me, but I couldn't (or wouldn't) see it unless it slapped me in the face; when it did slap me in the face, the guilt made me crave more drugs. Anything that added to my already overwhelming guilt and shame was too much for me. The high from drugs helped lift the guilt and shame.

One lonely night, after walking the streets all day, I called my mom. I must've been in my late twenties. I don't remember why I called her but I was tired; I was so tired.

She said, "Hello."

I said, "Mom," and went on to explain why I called, but she cut me off.

"Ruth, is that you? Where are you Ruth? When are you coming home? I walk around this house and I see the things you made and Ruth it feels like you died." She was sobbing on the phone.

I was crying too but didn't want her to know it. I didn't know what to say. I ended up saying, "I'm not dead mom."

By then I was high most of the time, which numbed me emotionally. When I wasn't high, the desperation for more drugs gave me tunnel vision. Drugs were everything to me.

The victim mindset and the desperation of getting more drugs blinded me from seeing what was right in front of me. I didn't want to see it.

CHAPTER TEN

Another Baby Step

When I got out of jail in 1983, at age twenty-nine, I had no choice but to go back to the same life. There were times when I just started walking after being released, with nowhere to go, so I relied on what I knew to do.

Bridges with family, friends, and even rehabilitation centers were severed. By the time I was finally able to escape "the life," I had been to four different in-patient rehabs, to no avail.

A male staff and I "had an affair" while I was living at one of the rehab centers. I was hoping his "feelings for me" would intensify and he would leave his wife and family for me. It never happened.

I didn't get rehabilitated either. How could I, when authority figures were really predators in disguise? It's not only pimps who were willing to use me for their own benefit under the guise of "being helpful." Even professionals who were supposed to help me saw me as easy prey because, after all, she's in "the life" by choice. Therefore, being preyed upon continued.

At age thirty-four, I signed up for the methadone program. Methadone is a legal drug that is distributed by clinics to help drug addicts break their addictions to opiates.

At the time, I thought it was worthwhile because it was free and it was a drug I didn't have to sell myself for. I had half a mind to get clean, but I mostly signed up for the program because methadone offered a better high than the drugs on the street. Dealers cut pure heroin with other chemicals in order to have more to sell and therefore make more money. Cutting pure heroin with other chemicals was necessary to avoid overdoses and deaths but it weakened the high, too.

Drug addicts can easily develop immunity to methadone. After a while, they don't feel the effects of it and don't get a high anymore. They still need to take it, however, to fend off physical withdrawal symptoms. Many end up having to be weaned off of it. For some, it's a lifetime prescription, because withdrawal from methadone can be fatal – withdrawal from methadone is more severe than withdrawal from street-cut heroin.

Today, I think methadone treatment is a total farce. How can giving someone a drug help them break their drug addiction? I suppose it *can* help with opiate withdrawals, but for me, quitting cold turkey allowed for a spiritual awakening. Of course, we are all different and everybody's rock bottom is different too.

Even when I was part of the methadone program, I kept using street drugs.

Henry let me use his car and I traveled 30 miles daily, with three others, to get my methadone. After being on the program for a certain period of time, we could pick up a week's worth. If patients were on the program long enough, they were "upgraded" to the maintenance program and only had to come to the clinic once a month. Leaving the clinic with so much methadone allowed us to sell it to other addicts; many did that when it didn't give them a high anymore.

To be on the program, clients had to see one of their counselors every week and drop urine for drug testing. I complied and saw my counselor once a week, but I quickly learned how to cheat on the drug tests.

In order for any rehabilitation to be effective, a trust between the drug addict/human trafficking victim and counselor/advocate must be established. I wanted to trust so badly that I was reckless when it came to who I trusted. I was never taught to be careful and I never practiced good judgment on who to open up to.

I spilled my guts to my counselor and vented all my frustrations and anger. He responded many times with silence, and then he would compliment me on how I looked. I felt he was minimizing my issues, but he was still my counselor who must know what he was doing. I longed for his wise counsel, but I figured it just took time to get acquainted. But as time went on, he never went any deeper. He listened as I vented during our sessions, but the feedback I got from him was usually superficial. I soon saw him as someone I just needed to sit with in order to get my methadone.

But every time he made a comment about what I was wearing or told me I looked "hot," I wondered, "Is he flirting with me? Is he in love with me?" When I pointed out that I was too fat in my thighs, he responded by saying, "Ruth, it's like when you go shopping for a car. You see a car that's in good shape, even though it has a small dent in the front fender, you buy it anyway because it's still a good looking car, right?" I appreciated his attempts to boost my ego. I didn't get many compliments from "squares," so I took it as wise counsel. To those with the victim mindset, a mere compliment can reel them in. I'm sure it was obvious how little I thought of myself, and he knew I was easy prey.

After being on the program for six months, he made sexual advances during one of our sessions. Of course, this kind of thing was routine to me and no big deal at the time, so I went along with it for a while, but I soon sensed deceit. I expected more from him because he was my counselor. He was supposed to be concerned about my welfare and my future. I expected a better feeling with this guy, but it wasn't feeling good anymore. He wouldn't kiss me or hold me like I expected him to, and because he was my counselor, I didn't see him as a sex deal or a "date."

All counselors at the clinic had to document their clients' progress. If the counselor didn't think the client was making progress, or if the client had skipped too many sessions, the counselor could withhold the methadone until the client was compliant. So I was compliant. Instead of counseling sessions, we had sex. Unlike the others, he agreed to safe sex. He was also concerned about his safety regarding the other staff becoming too suspicious, so he coached me on how to cover for him. "Now just be cool on your way past the receptionist; act like everything is normal. Just say 'good night' and walk out."

I felt used.

Other clients could pick up their dose and leave, but the ones I rode with had to wait because I had to see my counselor first. They kept asking why my counselor was being so strict with me. I told them I didn't know why, but I started to see my counselor as the one standing in my way of feeding my habit. Also, even if I wanted to actually get rehabilitated, I didn't have a chance with him. I got angry.

I decided he was not going to get away with it anymore, so I went to the director of the clinic and told him what was going on. He asked me to take a lie detector test. The staff gathered near the door where the test was taking place, anxiously waiting to hear the results. When I emerged from the room, the conductor of the test revealed the results to them: I'd passed.

They all gasped in disbelief. There was a big commotion and the women were crying. All their faces were angry— angry with me! I was struck with confusion. *Are all the counselors phony? Is no one on my side?*

They found it so hard to believe that their co-worker, a respected counselor, could be guilty of breaking the counselor/client boundaries and contract. Of course they saw me as someone who was not only incapable of speaking for herself, but was also discountable if she did speak up. Why would they believe a drug addict?

I know it's human nature to question whether a drug addict or a victim of any kind is telling the truth, but I'd passed the test. *They* had failed *me*. Even if they all felt their own jobs were on the line, isn't it the clients' welfare that's supposed to be their focus? They wouldn't have to fear losing their jobs if they were focused on clients. To me, it seemed like remaining client-focused during this crisis would be job security for them. At first, I'd thought it was just my counselor who was a sham, but now I doubted all of them. But then I second-guessed myself, again, and wondered if it was *me*. Was I was doing the right thing? I mean, counselors were supposed to give good advice for the addict to benefit from, right? Maybe they did have good reason to be angry with me. They were the mental health experts and they knew their feelings a lot better than I knew my own. I was confused and didn't know how to go forward.

Although I wasn't a strong enough person to stand up against a group of people, it was too late to go back now; I was up against all of them, whether I liked it or not. I had support from the others I rode with, and a few other addicts, and because of this, I felt I had to stay strong.

But even though the truth was evident, I still doubted my own judgment and questioned my decision to stand up to my counselor. I put myself second to everyone, constantly. I hadn't yet learned how to set boundaries. I always allowed my boundaries to be crossed, and this situation was no exception.

It did feel good to prove he was the one lying, though. He was just one more in a long line of people who'd read the word "victim" on my forehead and tried to take advantage of me. I chalked him up as just another "bad date" and put it behind me, but as time went on I had a change of heart.

It just wasn't sitting right with me, and I tried to honor my own gut feelings: I decided to sue the agency that conducted the clinic. To be honest, I was also thinking of the money. I wondered if a lawyer would see money in it too. When I first made the decision to seek a lawyer, I was focusing on honoring my gut feelings but my focus shifted to the money when the lawyer took the case.

Focusing on the money was only an outward need though. As time went on, I felt something inside me. I wasn't sure what it was but it sure felt good. I never went within and examined my heart before; but I couldn't ignore this inkling this time. It wasn't long after this when I came to realize that I wasn't only going to get money out of this, I was standing up for my dignity and THAT's what was feeling so good. Just being aware of my feelings was huge for me. I had set a boundary and stood by it! The pride that goes with standing up for me is what was tugging at my heart. It was another God wink.

God was winking at me as he held a door open and said, "Go ahead. Keeping going." And I did and I won my case.

It took many more years for me to learn to lean fully on the truth, listen to that voice inside me, but this was another important baby step in the right direction.

I don't mean to paint a picture that the clinic in whole was corrupt. The female counselor I had before the bad one left an impact on me. Her name was Sandra. She was a former addict herself, and conducted herself professionally. I was assigned to the other counselor after Sandra relocated and resigned.

Also, there was a male medic at the clinic who was proactive in his duties. Shortly after I signed up for the program, I was notified that this medic had passed me in the hallway and noticed open sores on my arms. He put in an order for me to be checked for syphilis. It was positive and I was successfully treated for it. His knowledge and quick thinking were what I needed to prevent the disease from progressing. I appreciate that he saw to it that his duties were carried out professionally, and according to protocol.

The legal process dragged on. I continued in "the life" and was still addicted. I got busted again, in 1989. I was thirty-four years old. My lawyer in the civil suit had to come to the jail to discuss the out-of-court settlement the clinic offered. I told my lawyer to take it. Because I was arrested for drugs, and in jail, the lawyer thought taking the out-of-court settlement was a good idea, too.

It was a small amount of money, but it was enough to maybe start anew. I had had enough and I wanted out.

I'd been living this life for seventeen years, and I was sick and tired of being sick and tired all the time. I had lost everyone who had ever cared for me, and everything I'd ever valued.

I thought of my family the most during that six months in jail. I knew I couldn't count on them when I got out. The first five times I was in jail, they wrote me letters about God, and they begged me to get help. By this sixth time, they'd given up on that approach and their letters had become warnings to stay away from Mother.

During this stint in jail, I made yet another decision to get out of "the life." I didn't get visitors, except for the ladies who came to the jail to conduct church services for us.

I broke the news to Henry that I didn't need him anymore. I surprised myself when I actually got these words out. I wasn't sure if I'd ever need him again, but I took a leap of faith and severed my relationship with him. It felt so good! This time, I was serious about starting anew when I got out of jail.

Still, it took a few more visits before Henry really got the message. He disregarded what I'd said, at first. I'm amazed at the courage it took for me to stand firm until the relationship was finally severed. I give myself a lot of credit for that, because I didn't have another source of money to take his place once the lawsuit money ran out. The money I got from the lawsuit wasn't much but it WAS enough to start anew.

My vet brother, Jerry, made one last attempt to encourage me. His letter read, "Ruth, you have tried everything there is to try in life; why not try God?" I read it over and over. I thought about the day my mom and Ken had me in that "prayer lock" and how I'd walked away from them feeling so alone because they said I couldn't come back.

I remembered the Christian counselor when I was younger telling me that I was forgiven, but I wasn't sure if I really was. I relived the apple orchard rape in my head over and over in jail. I remembered what the nice detective had said, that I hadn't asked for this kind of life. I wondered whether anyone else had that same hunch. I reflected on the time when my brother, Ken, drove by me while I was standing on a street corner. Oh, how sick I was of it all.

The church ladies seemed to have so much peace. I wanted this peace, so during a service, I asked one of them, Char, what the name of her church was. She told me the name and, to my surprise, it was the same church my brothers attended. I asked her if she knew them.

She was shocked. "Well, yes, I know them. What happened to you? Why are you here?"

I was embarrassed, but she was nice. I avoided the question and was vague in my answer and she didn't press me for any more information, but I worried that she would at some point; I considered avoiding her by not going to any more church services. I always worried about starting a genuine relationship with anyone who's not in "the game" because they couldn't be trusted with knowing that I was a street girl. This was also why I would never get married, not to a square anyway. I saw them all as judgmental people who were not on my side. But after visiting with the church ladies in jail, I could see they had peace and I didn't. So who was really the square here, me or them?

Char and I started writing letters. She was so nice to me. She brought me books and other items and never again asked what I'd done wrong that landed me in jail. She looked beyond the surface and I felt a special bond with her. I didn't want to break the bond by revealing the mess I was in. I certainly didn't want to scare her off because her kindness helped me do my time. She even told her daughter about me, and her daughter wrote to me, too. Her name is Laurie Johnson. They helped my sentence go by quicker. They sent me pictures and articles from magazines about puppies and other fun stuff. I was glad they didn't just give me Bible verses or lectures. I appreciated their time and efforts.

By the time the six months was up, I was feeling overwhelmed by how I was going to start over. I knew Henry wouldn't let me go. My credit was ruined. I hadn't graduated from high school. I thought if my family could take me back I'd be all set, because no one in the streets knew where my family lived (I'd been careful not to bring any street people home, especially the ones I feared). But without a safe place to go, I knew pimps and dealers would hound me and stalk me wherever I went.

Char had no idea what I was up against, but she was there to pick me up on my release date.

Wow! But where could she take me? I couldn't have her drop me off on the strip. She couldn't take me home to her house. *Now what do I do? Maybe I'll just ask her for a few bucks so I can get a cab and just let her go.* I did not want to disappoint her, but I couldn't come up with another way to handle this.

When I was released into the jail's parking lot, Char and I both saw a drug-dealing pimp waiting there for me, too. I didn't want to get in his car, but I figured I simply had to. She was scared when saw the pimp and I don't blame her because so was I. He was a shady and intimidating looking guy. He was giving us both the evil eye. He wanted me to believe that I still owed him money for drugs. I saw Char roll up her window and I thought she was going to take off and leave me there.

I'd had a few encounters with him in the past. He'd lured me into his car a few times, before I went to jail, by offering me free drugs. He was a reliable drug source for me for a little while, but I knew he wanted to be more than a drug source. He wanted me to work for him, but before he had the chance to zero in on me with his pimp tactics, I got busted. I didn't know how he knew my release date, but evidently he was determined to keep tabs on me.

Char didn't take off. She was waiting to see what I was going to do. I'll never forget her face. I was so moved by her display of loyalty because this woman was staying with me in my mess. God bless her for being there for me.

I told the drug-dealing pimp that I had to get rid of the church lady and that I'd meet him down on the strip in fifteen minutes and he fell for it. I got into the car with Char, and that was the beginning of my new life.

She took to me to my mother's house, where she and my mother talked for a long time. To this day, I don't know what that conversation was like. Later in life I asked my mother, but she would never talk about it. I regret that I never had the chance to ask Char about it before she died.

CHAPTER ELEVEN

The Beginnings Of Change (Or, Starting Over Stinks)

om took me back in. I was thirty-four and she was sixty-one.

I think Char's persuasion convinced Mother to take me back against my brothers' and sisters' wishes. When I think about this, I'm apt to think that my mother must have opened up to Char. Mother was usually so determined to never allow herself to "be seen," so she never opened up to anyone. She never even opened up to any of her close friends. I think Char must have moved her with her love and acceptance, like she'd moved me. I think Mother could see that Char was staying with us in all of our mess, too. I think Mother opened up to her and confided in her like she could never do with anyone else. Char was heaven-sent.

I had the lawsuit money, so I didn't have to rely on her financially. I bought a car and was able to support myself while I looked for work. The only wrinkle was that, whenever my siblings came to Mother's house, I had to take all my things to the basement and hide from them. I kept all my belongings in a box. She'd promised them that she would let me go and stop enabling me, so I tried to keep it a secret that I was living there.

But I couldn't hide my presence there for very long—and I didn't want to. I was staying clean and looking for work. Soon, I started cooking Sunday dinners for my siblings when they came over, but I got the cold shoulder from them even long after they "allowed" me to come back around our mother.

I enrolled in a computer class at a local Community Education Center and went on to get my GED. I attended Alcoholics Anonymous and Narcotics Anonymous meetings, and began sessions with Ken Navis, the Christian counselor that my mother had taken me to when I was younger. I don't think he was trained in trauma-related issues, but he was a key player in opening my eyes nonetheless. I never told him about my life as a "hooker." I couldn't. I didn't want him to see me as beyond redemption. I didn't want to disappoint him. I figured he would see that my issues were just too bizarre to treat and then he'd give up on me.

He listened to me patiently as I went on and on about how trapped I felt. The patience he displayed told me I was a priority to him at every session. He often asked, "Can you tell me more about that?" or "Can you elaborate on that?" or "What do you think of that?" Even though I whined a lot, he encouraged me to keep talking, to go within and examine my own feelings and beliefs. I knew he was in for the duration. He was truly interested in my feelings and beliefs. I know now that he was also trying to change the thoughts and beliefs I had about myself: he wanted me to believe, with all my heart, that I was just as worthy of forgiveness as the next person. I argued back relentlessly and tried to come up with all kinds of evidence to prove him wrong, to prove that I was beyond redemption.

Even though I turned all of his suggestions into arguments, he kept listening. He listened more than he spoke and when he did speak, he validated my fears and feelings. He shared some of the times when he'd felt the same way I did. This made me feel safe enough with him to open up a bit more. I decided to I come out with some confessions to see what he would say, but only bits and pieces at first. I couldn't just spill my guts. I'd been duped by counselors before, so I had to "test the waters" a bit more.

Unloading is what victims need to do to be able to heal and move forward, but they are reluctant to do this because they don't want to drain anyone or burden them. They fear they will only end up having to manage another's shock, pity, or scorn, so they hold back. You have to gain their trust and it takes time to do that. The more patient you are with them, the more time you give them, the better the chances are that they will open up to you.

My counselor responded to my confessions by saying, "Yes, you made some mistakes, but they are forgivable mistakes Ruth." He pointed to a framed picture on his wall that read, "Just because you made mistakes, doesn't mean you ARE a mistake." He continued, "You are not the only one in this world who made mistakes. Others have made even worse mistakes than this but they are forgiven, just like you are."

Most trafficking victims are ashamed of what they did to survive, like cooperating with rapists because their life was on the line, or using drugs to endure the pain. When they DO disclose this to you, respond by praising them for using these strategies because these strategies are probably what saved their life. Dr. Brené Brown says "shame cannot survive being spoken". Releasing the shame helps victims move forward and on to becoming victors.

I argued back. "I will never get a job. I don't have any skills and no one will hire anyone like me. Who would ever trust a drug addict?"

He said, "Not so fast. You are not a drug addict anymore and there's a lot of forgiving people in this world. I believe God has just the right, forgiving employer waiting for you right now, but Ruth it's up to you to go out and find that employer. I can see that you have what it takes to make it in life. I believe in you. I believe there's an employer out there who will believe in you too, but YOU have to believe in you." He continued with a motivational kind of tone in his voice and said, "Show the world what you can do Ruth. There's a power inside of all of us, including you, that you need to tap into. Don't ignore it. Ignoring it is what will hold you back; not what other people do or think. It depends on what YOU do. It's your decision."

After many sessions of arguing with him about my potential and worth, he finally looked at me one day and said, "Ruth, I want you to write down everything that you're ashamed of. Write down everything that you don't think you'll ever be able to make amends for and bring that list to your next appointment." He gave me my appointment card and said, "See you next week."

I did not like that idea. How could I show him my shame? I was a bit confused about how this would help me, but I wrote a list because I was beginning to trust him. At the same time, I worried that after he read what I wrote, he would see me as "one of them," or as one who was beyond his reach.

I also worried that I could cause *him* to feel inadequate—after all, my issues were just too bizarre to treat. Again, I put myself second. I was so used to worrying about my traffickers' and abusers' emotions and moods that it became first nature for me to do it with others. This was my blind spot for a long time.

Little did I know that it was this very blind spot that was holding me back. Victims transform to victors when they see themselves as being worthy enough to receive genuine support without feeling obligated to pay it back or do something in return.

I didn't write down *everything* on the list. It was daunting to write it, nonetheless. Writing down my shame meant writing down what was on my police record (except for the prostitution charges; I still didn't trust him *that* much).

I figured that when he saw that I had a criminal record, he'd know how hopeless it really was for me, and I guess I was hoping I'd win the argument and prove that I didn't stand a chance of being hired anywhere for a long time. My criminal record was like a big ugly scar that everyone could see. I wanted him to see that it was the charges on my police record that were holding me back in life, that it was this ugly scar that was holding me back in life, not my beliefs.

When it was time to go back for my next session, I wasn't sure I could look him in the face. *Should I even go in? Can I let myself be seen like this?* Then, I just put one foot in front of the other and went in.

I was filled with emotion as I handed him the list. He took it from my hand and held onto it for a few seconds. He then turned to look at me and you know what he did then? He ripped it up! He never even read it! As he was ripping it up, he said, "It doesn't matter what you've done Ruth. You're forgiven."

He didn't even have to know what the list said. He didn't even read it. He definitely wasn't looking for information to use against me or help him exploit me. I was shocked and started asking about some of the specifics on the list.

He quickly interrupted me. "No! There are no ifs, ands, or buts about it. It's all forgiven. You can forget about all that now." He let all the little pieces fall into the wastebasket. "It's time to plan out a job search for you and look to the future. What do you say? God has a job out there waiting for you, Ruth, and we need to find it."

My eyes filled with tears. I was so moved. I could tell this man believed what he was saying: that I'm forgiven and that I could get a job. No man had ever extended so much patience and acceptance to me before. I know he didn't see "scum of the earth" in me. He responded to me as a whole person, like Char did, and like the kind detective did. Even though I was relentless in proving my unworthiness, he never took anything personally. He wasn't interested in the gory details and he let me talk about whatever I wanted to vent about as he patiently listened. I thank God for him.

We practiced what I would say at job interviews. He was the one who eventually convinced me to just tell the truth instead of reciting good lines to say. He said, "The truth will set you free."

In order to recover, victims need to know you will stay with them in their mess. Knowing they have a trusted person who will walk along side of them—not in front of them, not behind them, but right alongside them—empowers them. Knowing that someone trusted me and believed in me was huge for me. I felt true acceptance the day my list was ripped up. It was such a powerful moment. I left his office that day motivated like never before. *I just might be able to do something with my life after all.* I felt that power inside me once again.

———•———

I was almost there. I was letting this forgiveness thing take hold and I was starting anew while staying at Mom's house. I was getting impatient with my siblings, though. I wanted them to trust me again so badly, but it seemed like it was taking forever. My counselor asked me to be patient with them. I knew I was trustworthy and I was determined like never before to stay clean. I knew I was on my way to being a better sister and daughter; but they were not too sure yet.

The job search was going just as slowly. After each interview I filled my mom in on how it went—not well. I got discouraged and told her there was no use. I was convinced no one would hire me. I truly believed I was a slow learner and that I just didn't have what it takes. I thought my chances of being employed were slim.

Mother consoled me and gave me pep talks to keep me going. She would say, "You are so pretty and intelligent. You can do anything with your life. Why not put it on your application that you can speak Spanish? I'm sure employers can use bilingual people."

This was a big change of attitude for Mom. She had often expressed disappointment in my ability to speak Spanish instead of Dutch, but now her attitude seemed to be more accepting. My Spanish skills were not good, but she didn't know that. When she heard me speak Spanish, it sounded good to her, but others who understood the language could see there was a lot of room for improvement.

I didn't believe I was pretty or intelligent. I thought she was just saying that to make me feel good and to boost me up so the hell my drug use had caused would end.

I don't know how she went from being so abusive to becoming so encouraging, but I liked it. I thought back on all those times she'd called me names and told me I would never be any good. What a difference! Maybe she could see that her put-downs played a role in my low opinion of myself. Maybe she wanted to make up to me for not being there for me. Maybe she just wanted her own suffering to end. I wasn't sure, but I was not going to buck it.

CHAPTER TWELVE

Deciding Is Not Enough

No matter how much I practiced for interviews, and no matter how many great lines I used, I still couldn't make a good enough impression on employers to land a job. I'm sure it was because of my police record.

Finally, I took my counselor's advice and just told the truth. I applied for a job as a cashier at a gas station that had just been built. Only the gas pumps and the convenience store were open; the bay for oil changes was still under construction. I told the interviewer that I had had a drug problem; but that I was getting my life straightened out and that I really needed a job. I was hired. That's when I learned to lean on the truth: the truth really will set you free. This was a huge boost for me. I attempted to start a new life and someone gave me a second chance! Knowing that someone was putting their trust in me was so empowering. I felt I had the motivation and determination now to go forward and show the world what I could do.

I was on my way!

But old habits are so hard to break, especially old thought

habits. Breaking the embedded stinking thinking is one of the most difficult tasks a PTSD victim, a drug addict, or anyone with an issue will undertake.

Things were going well, but I was still discouraged by how slow progress with my siblings was going. I was expecting a pat on the back from them and it wasn't coming fast enough. I wanted them to sing my praises from a mountain top for the progress I'd made—to me, the progress I'd made was huge and I didn't want them to minimize that. I wanted to be trusted right away.

Instant gratification was first nature to me. I was still living with Mom and still struggling to save money so I could get out on my own. Plus, learning to think positively and learning to be patient was like learning a second language; it was so hard and it was taking so long.

It took two grueling years of patience to get my siblings back. They finally did forgive me, and I thank God for them, but before they finally came around, I had lost patience. I started thinking of all the bad I had done and all the bad that was done to me. Doubts about this forgiveness thing crept in.

I hadn't yet fully grasped how forgiving yourself and others was not a one-time thing, but a work in progress. I hadn't yet learned how to practice mindfulness. Mindfulness is being aware of your thought patterns, recognizing the negative thoughts, noticing how and when they creep in, and then knowing how to discard them.

Knowing how to discard those negative thoughts was the kicker. I was more aware of my thoughts and feelings, but I hadn't yet learned to discard the negative thoughts and replace them with positive ones.

How do I make the bad thoughts and memories go away? How do I shed this heavy load of guilt and shame?

I learned a lot from Narcotics Anonymous (NA) meetings.

There are twelve steps in NA and Alcoholic Anonymous (AA) that members have to comply with in order to make their recovery successful. I believe these steps can also help one recover from the victim mindset. I believe the 12 steps of NA and AA (and others of course) are principles we all should live by.

Step number eight and nine hit home with me right away. Number eight cites: Make a list of all persons we had harmed, and be willing to make amends to them all. Number nine cites: Make direct amends to such people wherever possible, except when to do so would injure them or others.

If I didn't follow these steps, I knew I would not be able to go forward. I had come to forgive myself, but I really wanted to be forgiven by my family. I didn't think I could go forward without their forgiveness. I knew I needed to make amends to them and to others that I hurt, but how could I make amends when no one would give me a chance to? I found myself blaming them for holding me back. I made *them* the reason why I was not able to go forward. Blaming was first nature to me and I was slipping back into "stinking thinking."

I had made tremendous strides already but there was more I needed to learn about that voice inside me and power I held inside. After being clean for about two years, working at the gas station as a cashier, and still staying with Mom, I gave in to the stinking thinking (aka, temptation). I stayed in a drug house for three days getting high, without any food or sleep.

It all started as I was on my way downtown. I saw the old gang hanging out on a corner. I thought, *If only they could see me now. I'm drug free and I look a lot better than I did the last time they saw me. I want to show off a little bit. It'll be good for me.*

I stopped and yukked it up with the ol' gang for a bit and the solace of being back in my comfort zone was immediate.

During the last part of my drug use, my appearance reflected the abuse. I looked pretty bad; I weighed ninety-nine pounds and there were little scabs all over my arms and face. I wanted to stop and show off my new look, show off that I had a car, and brag a little about being drug-free. But those bonds built over years of doing drugs together were stronger than I'd thought. It was just so easy to be with them, and so easy to make them happy. I still had a little money in my savings account from the lawsuit; they jumped in my car and we went to an ATM. I withdrew all my money and we scored (bought drugs).

On the third day of my cocaine binge, while getting high in a bedroom with five dealers and users, I heard glass breaking. It sounded like it was coming from the kitchen. I shrugged it off as just hearing things from the effects of too much cocaine.

Then I heard it again, and then again. It was getting louder and louder. I heard a woman yell, "Ruth! Ruth!" I could tell the others heard it, too, by their startled facial expressions, so I knew it wasn't just me. Everyone jumped into position and a couple of guys guarded the door.

I heard, "Ruth! Ruth!" again, and this time I recognized my mother's voice. I couldn't believe it. I blurted out, "It's my mother!"

One of the men put his hand on his gun and told me, "You'd better get rid of her because I am not going to jail today." I needed to get out of that room so I could protect my mother, but they wouldn't let me out. Then there was banging on the door of the room we were in. My mother and another man were talking on the other side; I begged them to let me out. They had their guns out. I feared for my mother. I had to prevent the worst from happening.

I pleaded with them. "I can't get rid of her unless you let me out of here." They couldn't deny it, so they finally let me out. As soon as the door opened, my mother started hitting the man who opened the door, in his chest. I had to drag her away from him before he hurt her.

The young Mexican man my mother was with was a stranger to me. He looked like a nice, clean-cut guy who was in over his head; when he saw the guns drawn, he took off running.

Thank God that I got my mother out of there, and that she succeeded in getting me out of there. She was parked across the street and we got in her car and left.

I was taken aback by her strength and tunnel vision. It was surreal. She had to have known how dangerous it was to do what she did, but she was focused on one outcome and went for it, despite the danger or consequences she may have had to face.

She scowled at me. "You high on that shit again?"

I said nothing, in part because the drug's effects wouldn't allow me to speak, and also because I was so shocked and so ashamed, but at the same time, so relieved to be out of there. Deep down, I felt valued because my mother saw me as worth fighting for.

The next morning, after resting, eating and allowing the drugs to wear off, my emotions were very raw. I have never felt so much remorse in my life. After two whole years of progress under my belt, I threw it all away. And for what?

Abusing drugs was a daily routine for me in the past and I thought nothing of it; but this time was different. How could I do such a thing and throw away everything I had gained? It was a hard lesson to learn but I learned from it. That was the last time I did drugs.

Mother told me I'd better call my boss and do some fast talking to save my job. I had no idea what I could possibly say to my boss that would keep her from firing me. I didn't even want to make the call.

It was useless, I figured, but Mother hounded me to make the call. "You never know. They might be desperate for you to come back. Now get on the phone! On the phone! You need a job. Call your boss!"

I made the call while in the same room with Mother. I wanted her to hear the conversation so I could prove to her how useless it was.

When I heard my boss answer, I said, "Anita? This is Ruth."

I was about to say more, but she cut me off and said, "Oh, Ruth, I'm so glad you were able to get through. I know you must have been sick and our phones have not been working for the last three days. How are you doing now?"

It took me by complete surprise. I hesitated a moment before saying, "Well, I'm doing fine now and I'm wondering if you needed me to come in today."

She said, "No, not today, but can you be here first thing in the morning?"

I said, "Certainly, I will see you then."

I did not deserve luck like that, but I wasn't going to blow this chance. Today I know this wasn't just luck. It was another "God wink." God was winking at me as He held the door open for me to pass through, as if to say, "I've got you covered."

Mom and I were so relieved. I felt hopeful again, but I also knew I had a long road ahead of me. Not only would I have to start all over, but I also had to make up for the ridiculous and senseless relapse. I'd made a huge step forward in progress, but went two huge steps back with the relapse.

My mother never said much about rescuing me from the drug house. Years later, she told me that she had paid the young Mexican man to help her rescue me. That was the only thing she ever explained about that day, but I knew, deep down, that she wanted to make it up to me for not being there for me in my childhood. She made me swear to secrecy about it. I couldn't understand her request, but I honored it.

Today I wonder whether the conversation she had with Char, on the day I was released from jail, had anything to do with her vowing to fight for me. I think Char helped her see how much she needed to be there for me, and not just by offering me a place to stay. I'm apt to think Char got my mother thinking about things, and that Mother didn't like the thought of dying with so many regrets.

I know Mother had no one else to talk to about her daughter, because talking about me would mean that she would have to admit that I was a jail bird and a drug addict and she was afraid others would see how she failed me. She'd intended to guard this shameful secret with her life, just like I hid mine. Char already knew our shame story and maybe Mother saw Char as the one she could open up to. I don't know, but that's my theory.

Mother had always had a hard time expressing love to me, but the day she rescued me from the drug house her message of love was loud and clear. No words were necessary. It was what I needed from her. I finally got what I needed from her! I feel guilty for putting her in that kind of danger, even though it was really her choice. Guilty, but grateful.

I kept this a secret until she was seventy-two, when I wanted my siblings to understand why I defended this woman we'd all suffered under for so long.

It took me years of being clean from drugs and years of therapy, as well as the switch of Mom becoming dependent on me, for me to really register the effects of being abused by her. She'd been severely abused, raped and beaten by her husband for years. This helped me understand her emotional unavailability, her mixed signals, her cruelty to her own children—understand, but not excuse.

I was eventually able to look beyond her behavior, like my siblings did with me. Even more, I was able to relate to her. She, too, dealt with a heavy burden of shame. She often told people that her husband died because she could never admit she was a divorced woman. Even when filling out forms that asked for marital status, she'd cover up her answer in fear of anyone seeing that she checked the box that said, Divorced.

When I realized that her poor decisions and choices in raising us stemmed from her own years of neglect and abuse, I finally stopped blaming her. I just wish she'd gotten counseling to help her deal with the abuse, the rapes, the shame, but she never did.

The day my mother rescued me from the drug house was truly the last day of my drug life.

CHAPTER THIRTEEN

People Can Change

When I was thirty-six, still staying with Mom and working at the gas station, a customer came in who I recognized: Julio, a Cuban drug dealer to whom I still owed fifty dollars.

Would he recognize me? I did look a lot healthier, and many from my recent past did not recognize me anymore, which was a blessing. I had learned from counseling that my judgment on who I allowed in my life was impaired and needed improvement, so I tried to avoid people from my past. I couldn't tell who was for me, and who was against me. I would trust without testing.

Julio picked up his purchase and got in line to check out. He was with another man and they were both speaking Spanish. I tried to make out what they were saying and heard Julio tell the other man that he knew the cashier. I cringed and wondered if anyone could tell I was nervous. I thought for sure he was going to ask me for the fifty bucks.

When it was his turn to check out, he put his purchase on the counter and, to my surprise, he spoke to me in English. The last time I'd seen him, eight years earlier, he only spoke Spanish.

He asked me if I recognized him. I didn't want my co-workers or boss to grasp our conversation, so I spoke in Spanish and told him I did, indeed, recognize him. He was pleasantly surprised that I could speak Spanish.

He told me he had done seven years in prison and had been out for a year. He went on to tell me he was starting a new life of freedom: working an honest job, no more drug dealing. His semi-truck was parked in the gas station's parking lot.

It was so cool to hear that; I wanted to hear more. I wanted to tell him about my decision to stay clean too, so when he asked me out to dinner, I agreed.

It was a wonderful night. He had a tough reputation in the drug world before he went to prison; no one dared cross him, including me. He and his family were my main suppliers for a long time. Now I was seeing another side to him. What a difference! I knew people could change because I had. I was so excited to have run into him again, in this way, and not in the streets. We both shared the desire to live a clean life.

He saw a different side of me, too. I didn't spill my guts about too much of my past, mostly because I didn't need to; he already knew most of it. He made it clear that my past didn't matter. He was very accepting and forgiving. He made me feel special; like no other man in my life had. I shared my dreams and goals with him. He said he wanted to be a part of that. Julio knew Carlos and he said he could offer me a much better life than Carlos had. That night, I fell in love.

We saw each other often. I brought him to Mom and she liked him, too. I loved to watch Mom and Julio razz each other and share laughs. Julio was good to her and I appreciated that.

All was going well. Even my siblings seemed to take to Julio. They had started warming up to me and we seemed to be a family again. They had their own lives and struggles to deal with, but my brother Don reached out to me one Sunday when I made a Cuban feast for them at Mom's house. It was a dish called picadillo that Julio had taught me to make. Many of our dates consisted of just going to his place to cook Cuban food. Picadillo isn't a feast to Cubans (it's similar to hash), but my siblings enjoyed it. We sat around the table and chatted a bit after I had cleared the table. I was still nervous around my family because deep down I wondered what they thought of me. We weren't a family that had heart-to-heart talks, so I was always left to wonder how they really felt.

Don asked me if we had any more soda. I went to look and saw we had run out. We continued to chat and then Don did something that almost brought me to tears. I didn't want it to show because to him and to everyone else it was no biggie, but to me it was so moving. He took the keys to his Cadillac out of his pants pocket, put them on the table, and pushed them over to me, saying, "Hey, why don't you run to the store to get some more pop and pick up a pack of cigarettes for me on your way." What a huge sign that he trusted me. I got in his Cadillac and drove to the gas station where I worked and cried all the way there. It was what I needed from him. *Don trusts me!*

Julio and I were married a year later, in 1992, in the office of my Christian counselor. As far as I know, I was his second wife. I was thirty-seven and he was forty-six when we married and when I moved out of Mother's house.

His family was a little resistant to our marriage; my family wasn't too keen on it, either. I think both of our families were doubtful that an interracial marriage could succeed, but that didn't matter to either of us. In the past I was so sure I would never get married, especially to a "square." Julio wasn't in "the game" anymore and he wasn't a square. I thought he was a perfect fit for me.

Our marriage was great, at first. He was a great provider. He opened up to me about his life in Cuba and his childhood. It wasn't easy for him. Julio was one of ten kids. He came to the U.S. in 1980. He bragged about me to his friends and family, and even to people from our past, who knew of my "more shameful" past. All that felt great and I believed he was proud of me despite my past. Little did I know he was still attracted to the drug world and the people in it. He was showing me off as a way to impress THEM. Their view of him was still important to him.

My counselor, Ken Navis, asked me to give my testimony to some churches after Julio and I had been married for a few years. For about a year, I went around to area churches and gave my testimony. I spoke of my drug addiction and my recovery from it. I never spoke of being trafficked though. Human Trafficking wasn't even a phrase back then.

When mingling with the group after giving my testimony, many would comment on how surprised they were that I'd been a drug addict because I didn't "look the part." Well, I knew there were years when I *did* look like a drug addict. These comments brought me back to my counselor's office. He had words of hope on his walls in his office and one of them said, "Others can see joy in your face when you get a faith lift." So now when people tell me, "Ruth, you just don't look the drug addict type," I say, "That's because I had a faith lift." ☺

Julio attended my speeches at first, but my speaking schedule conflicted with his cross-country trucking trips, so I eventually went on my own. So many people were moved by my speeches and many would tell me about it afterwards. I enjoyed meeting them and it all felt very good, knowing I was helping others.

CHAPTER FOURTEEN

I'm Just Going To Be Me

My husband had a friend whose wife worked at a local clinic who said she would vouch for me, so I applied for a clerk position. When I was called in for an interview, I couldn't believe it. The job was better and more prestigious than I'd ever seen myself getting. I had my doubts about my abilities, but Julio encouraged me and helped me practice for the interview.

The truth had helped me land my gas station job, but I wasn't sure how it would work with different people. I was truthful on the application and I checked the box that asked if I had a criminal record.

The interviewer asked me about my criminal record and I was truthful: "All the offenses on my record stem from a drug addiction I now have a handle on." I told her how enthused I was to be drug-free. I emphasized the skills I had acquired from a computer class that I took while working as a cashier at the gas station. I told her I was a quick learner. I didn't think I was, but it sounded good.

She smiled and told me her husband was an alcoholic who got a lot of help and support from AA meetings. She said she could relate to my struggles and that she appreciated my honesty.

Oh, wow! I said to myself. This woman is a director of a clinic and married to an alcoholic? And she's admitting this to me? This proved to me once again we are all only human. Everyone has their own struggles in life and their own stories to tell.

We had a wonderful conversation, and after we talked for over an hour, I was hired.

In the space of several years, I'd gone from drug addiction and life on the streets to being a clerk at a clinic and wife to a man who had his own semi-truck. We were so happy. We built our own home; it was a lovely house. Julio could fix anything and was very proud of his skills. He loved working on cars and on his truck. He tried to help me "fix" my past, too.

We had enough money to help our families out financially. We disagreed on the amounts of money we sent to Cuba and the amounts of money we offered to my mother, but I always backed off and reasoned with myself that Cuba was a poor country.

While Julio was driving us down the strip one day, on our way downtown, we talked about how different the strip looked and about how happy we were that we were no longer a part of that scene. We got to a red light and a man pulled alongside of us. He rolled down his passenger-side window and then Julio rolled his window down. The man said, "Hello Ruth." I recognized him: it was Henry. He found out where I worked and kept calling me at the clinic. I'd told him to stop calling several times, but he kept it up.

When I told Julio who the guy was, he threw the car into park and got out. He grabbed the man's passenger door and shouted, "Look, you S.O.B., you don't know who you're messing with! Open this door!"

Henry sped off and Julio hopped back in the driver's seat and took off after him in hot pursuit. I asked Julio to back off and let him go. It took some convincing, but he finally did. Henry never called me again. Julio was my protector and hero. It felt so good to have this in my life. I loved him for it.

I was feeling good about myself. I'd proven that I really could do what I set out to do, that I really could change, and that people (even my family) would notice and treat me with respect. Still, I was nervous about co-workers or staff confronting me about my past or criminal history. I envisioned someone getting their hands on my written criminal history, confronting me with it, and saying, "A-ha! Explain this!"

While at my computer, I imagined that someone might post my past for everyone to see. How was I to ever going to prevent it? For years, it bothered me that I had no control over that. It influenced how I stood up for myself, and often, how I didn't. *If I stand up to anyone who bullies me, they could plaster my history on a billboard on the highway, or something, and I would be done.*

That was extreme thinking, I know. But that kind of thinking was a legacy of my PTSD, of my fear of judgmental people, and of the residual shame I still carried. It was a heavy load to carry, but I carried it in silence for years. For so long, I felt like a hypocrite because I was constantly working at hiding my true person. *"If they only knew..."* I'd say to myself over and over.

It was profoundly lonely not being able to make a true connection with other people because of the dark cloud that followed me wherever I went. I felt I was two-faced because I refused to let myself be seen.

Today I am proud to say that battle is over and done. I got counseling again, read a lot of self-help books, and joined support groups. As time went on, I learned I wasn't the only employee at the clinic with an ugly past. After hearing stories from other sur-

THE REALITIES OF HUMAN TRAFFICKING

vivors, I realized that, again, I needed to quit setting myself apart. Plus, I needed to stop overlooking the progress I had made and give myself the credit I deserved.

I know there will always be trolls in this world—folks who will try to bring me down. Not everyone is going to like me, and that's okay. I don't have to try to please everyone. It's too exhausting. I learned to lighten up on myself and give myself a well-needed break from keeping up appearances.

I'm just going to be me.

I was promoted to a lead position when I was forty-nine. I am so proud of my hard work. I have a deep sense of pride in my accomplishments because I didn't "sleep my way up." I "earned" a lot of money when I was in "the life," but I've earned so much more than that now, something so much more meaningful from my hard work and living an honest life. Remaining honest with myself and with others has gained me an inner peace that is so much more rewarding than any amount of money can buy.

Now, whenever I imagine being confronted by someone about my past, I envision myself saying, "Oh yea, but look at me now! I have an excellent credit score, an excellent employment history, many friends, and a loving family who back me up, and great Hallmark cards to prove it."

There are many people just like me. There are many who had it worse than me.

But I know where to get my strength: I know now that I'm not alone.

104

CHAPTER FIFTEEN

Survivor's Guilt

Even though I'm thankful to have survived, sometimes I feel guilty when I think of those who didn't make it.

While working at the clinic one day, Tracey, a girl I knew from street walked in to get the free condoms the clinic gave away. We'd become pretty good pals while on the street and we'd both wanted out of "the life." We'd talked about it many times.

When Tracey saw me at the clinic, she stopped dead in her tracks. We stared at each other in disbelief for several seconds. I hadn't seen her in a while and I could tell she was still out there; she was looking pretty bad. I could tell she was surprised at the way I looked too. She didn't have to say anything because I knew what she was thinking by the look in her eyes: she felt left behind. She saw I was doing well, but she was still trapped. I didn't know what to say. My heart went out to her.

She said, "Are you working here?" As if she couldn't already tell.

I said, "Yes, Tracey. I'm doing pretty well. I've been working here for a few years now."

She looked down at the floor, said, "Oh," then turned around and walked out the door.

I had a client waiting for me so I had to let her go. It was hard to watch her leave, because I knew she wanted to get off the dark path she was on.

Her head was hanging low as she walked away. My heart just ached for her.

Not long after that, I sat down to read the newspaper at home one day after work. I couldn't believe the headline: Tracey had been murdered.

Oh God!

Survivor's guilt grips me when I think of her. She died never being understood. She died never understanding herself.

I understand you, Tracey, and I'm so sorry I didn't take the time to talk to you more when you came to the clinic.

I have to do all I can to help who I can—for Tracey's sake, for my sake, for Mom's sake, and for goodness' sakes. I'm at a place in my life where I'm ready to give back. I have to make my life count. I'm not a throw-away or disposable person, like so many others thought I was, including me. Neither are any of the victims of rape or the sex trade.

In 1995, when I was forty, drug-free and still holding down a steady job, I took a different route home, because of construction and detours. I ended up going down the strip.

I hadn't been down the strip in years. It felt so strange to see it all again. I had many flash backs and my heart was bursting with thankfulness that I was lifted out of that mire.

Drunks were lying on the corners, just like when I was on that scene. Some of the buildings were boarded up and abandoned. There was a new generation of thugs on these streets. My heart sank as I saw how young they were. Then I saw a child standing on the corner that I used to stand on. She couldn't have been more than twelve years old. She was wearing a lot of makeup and a revealing outfit, but her clothes and make up did not hide her age. She was trying to do "her job," but she couldn't hide the fear on her face.

How could people just ride by her? Had the police seen this? I could not ignore it. I had to stop. I rolled down the passenger window as I approached her, and said, "Can I help you? Do you need a ride?"

She didn't respond. I thought maybe she couldn't hear me, so I spoke louder, but I soon realized why she wasn't responding. A man came up behind me and slammed his hands on my driver's side car window. He was angry, and shouted obscenities at me. I was torn over what to do. I knew he had this child under his control, but I was afraid of him. Calling the cops, back when I was on the corner, was not an option, and I knew it wasn't an option this time, either.

I had to drive away, but I drove back ten minutes later and saw her get into a car with another man. I didn't know who the man was, but my imagination went wild. I prayed he would help her.

Then I noticed a car behind me. It was the same man that had yelled obscenities at me, and there was another man with him. I bent the corner and proceeded to go home. They followed me. I got on the highway and they stayed right behind me. I had to lose them. I almost panicked, but I headed for the police station; after driving for about ten minutes, I realized they were gone.

Today, because of the laws that have been set in place to protect trafficked men, women, and children, I would call the police. Now I know I would have more back up to help girls like her.

CHAPTER SIXTEEN

Medical Consequences

I'd always figured that my past would prevent me from ever getting married. I didn't want to see any husband of mine always needing to defend me and have to work at hiding my past. Julio reassured me over and over that the past was the past but this was tested when I came home from work one day with some bad news: I have Hepatitis C.

My doctor didn't explain much about it when I was diagnosed; he only told me that there was no cure, that it was fatal, and that it was only contagious by blood. He told me I probably got it from a dirty needle.

My imagination went wild. I expected the worst: *Fatal? No cure? Am I going to die? Contagious? Did I pass it to my husband?*

I didn't know how I was going to tell my husband. The stigma about Hepatitis C was alive and well and I was convinced that this consequence of my past would be too much for him.

Julio asked me how the appointment went and I started to cry. I told him what the doctor found. He held me ever so lovingly and told me not to be afraid. "We will do this together. I am not afraid of any disease." Oh, how I appreciated his support. I was so thankful God had sent him into my life.

At the follow-up appointment, I was tested again, to eliminate any false positives. They also did other tests to learn what kind of Hepatitis C I had. In medical terms, the kind of Hepatitis C is referred to as the *genotype*. After all the testing, the doctor summed it up: "At this time there is no cure for Hepatitis C. There is a treatment called Interferon and Ribavirin, but there's only a thirty percent chance it will work for you. Your genotype is the most resistant to treatment, so it's up to you. The side effects are grueling. You could become anemic during treatment. If it gets too bad, we stop treatment. Hep C is fatal, but many live normal lives with it."

He added, "If you choose not to accept treatment, we want to test your blood every three months to monitor the alt levels. We can identify 'red flags' by checking the alt levels regularly. If they spike too high, it can be an indicator that your disease has progressed. It's a progressive disease and without treatment, it could progress to liver cancer."

When Julio and I left the doctor's office, I was in a daze. This was a lot of information to process. I had a big decision to make.

My husband consoled me and talked it over with me. I slipped into depression after it all sunk in. I even sat down and wrote my family a good-bye letter. I was convinced I didn't have much time to live. I couldn't focus on anything else. It was hard for Julio to see me so down, but I couldn't snap out of it. I went through the motions and went back to "keeping up appearances" to hide yet another shameful secret from the world: my filthy disease. I'm sure my experiences of having STDs at age eleven had a lot to do with why I felt so contaminated with Hep C.

As time went on I was able to accept the diagnosis and realized that it wasn't an immediate death sentence. I joined an online support group. I learned everything I could about the disease and my fears gradually subsided. I learned what to eat and what not to eat. I knew I had to abstain from drugs, both illegal and prescription, and from alcohol to protect my liver. I never did like alcohol, so that wasn't a problem.

The disease progresses very slowly, so the chances of dying from something else after living a long, normal life are great. I never did the treatment. There is a better treatment out there now with a higher success rate, with minimal side effects, but it's still too expensive. I'm told the cost will come down within a few months. I am so thankful I had Julio to help me through those hard times.

A few years after I was diagnosed with Hepatitis C, my husband came home with bad news: he had emphysema. He took it really hard.

I stood by Julio and did all I could to lift him up, like he did for me, but nothing helped. I would come home from work to find him lying on his stomach, on the living room floor; he wouldn't say anything. During this time, he applied for his permanent residence status with the US immigration, but he was denied because of his criminal history. He slipped into depression.

Again, there was no consoling him. He wouldn't do anything or say anything. It was so hard to see him like this. I felt helpless, but I had to be strong for him. The dream he'd had of the kind of life he intended to lead in the U.S. was disappearing, and it looked like he'd never get back to Cuba.

CHAPTER SEVENTEEN

My Gift To Julio

Julio longed for his family in Cuba, but if he'd gone there, the U.S. wouldn't let him back in because of his immigration status. After phone calls were disallowed between the two countries, we could only exchange letters. His children were having children and he knew he would never meet his grandchildren.

After writing many letters to his family and learning all I could about Cuba, I offered to go there in his place. Julio loved the idea. I was afraid to go alone but I wanted to be strong and brave for him. It took a year to get my passport and wait for my job to allow me to take vacation.

Because of the embargo that the U.S. had against Cuba, Americans couldn't freely travel there, but people who had family in Cuba could travel legally there once a year.

"Who knows if I'll even make it back to the U.S.?" went through my mind while in Cuba. I tried not to focus on that, but it was impossible.

I did make it back to the U.S., after spending ten days in Cuba. I don't regret the trip because it was quite an experience, but going to Cuba was not a wise decision on my part.

Bonds were formed between me and some of Julio's family. I took seven hours of family videos, which ended up being the last time Julio saw his kids and grandkids. When I returned to Miami, Julio and I spent three days in front of the screen, watching the videos in our pajamas. It felt good to have been able to "bring them together," even if only on a screen.

I loved the kids in Julio's family. Their excitement in meeting and talking with the American was so cute. They made me feel like a celebrity. But just because I was American they listened intently to everything I said and that concerned me.

Because of this I tried to leave each one with a thought to ponder about their self-worth. They thought I was bigger than life and I wanted them to have a more realistic view of foreigners and themselves.

"Mija recuerde, nadie es mejor que tú, ningun Ameriano ni ningún Cubano. Tu eres tan valiosa como el que más. *My dear, remember: no one is better than you, not any American, nor any Cuban. You are as valuable as anyone else.*"

Julio's brother, Samuel, and his wife worked hard to ensure my safety and satisfaction while I was there. I saw Samuel evaluate the situation constantly to make sure I had everything I needed, and that I was not bothered by others or by all the attention I was getting. He was my bodyguard and confidant. Later, when I left Cuba, saying good-bye to Samuel and his wife at the airport was the hardest. They were so reliable and loving.

I never shook the feeling that I was stupid for going there. I did the "what if" thing a lot. I thought of the warnings I'd read in travel chat-rooms on the internet. The U.S. State Department told me I'd be on my own if anything happened to me there. During the planning, I didn't give it much thought because Julio and his family told me over and over that I would have no problems, but once I was there, I worried.

The lesson I learned from my trip to Cuba is that I was too trusting, and still too needy. My offer to go to Cuba was too self-sacrificing.

There is a fine line between being compassionate and being a victim. When navigating through life with the victim mindset, one is robbed of ever knowing true compassion and of ever reaping the rewards of giving.

Dr. Brene Brown says, "Compassion without boundaries isn't compassion."

Survivors of trafficking need to know that if you don't do the hard work of understanding how the dynamics between you and the traffickers played a key role in you falling prey in the first place, you can blindly walk into situations of being used and abused all over again. The push and pull dynamics between trafficker and victim happens every day with everyday people in everyday life.

Cuba didn't have the comforts of home for me. It certainly was not a vacation for me—it was more of a vacation for them. I supplied all the money we needed for gas, food, liquor, and parties.

At the time, I saw myself as the kind of person who could adjust well to any environment; I saw this as a virtue. Now that I'm sixty, I can see I was just too accustomed to putting my own feelings aside or even ignoring them all together. I still had a lot of work to do on myself.

If I had paid attention to my own feelings, I never would have gone. I was so busy focusing on what others wanted and desired, that I didn't even ask myself what I wanted and desired.

My mother used to brag to her friends about how I always

felt sorry for others. I thought feeling sorry for others, no matter what, is what made me a compassionate person, but in reality it left me vulnerable and open to being used, taken advantage of, and victimized.

CHAPTER EIGHTEEN

My Protector No More

Our marriage was great at first, but he had his inse-curities and I was still very needy. I needed a lot of reassurance. We *did* help see each other through tough times, especially with our health problems, but there were times when I wondered if he was really sincere. His insecurities showed a lot of the time.

I learned later he had been cheating on me. Today, I won-der whether he already had another woman when I was diagnosed with Hep C. Now that I look back, I can see that I still had blinders on. Not as bad as before but I failed to see that I was not being re-spected. I was unknowingly trying hard to manage his manipula-tions and demands. Julio was clear on what he thought my role as a wife was from the beginning: I was to obey and he was to lead. I always thought I could live with that. When he got angry and seemed out of control, I figured that if I just tried harder he would calm down and we would be in love again. I think what really kept our marriage together was that I thought I did well at managing his emotions. Now I know it's impossible to manage another's emotions. Trying to do the impossible is exhausting. No one can make another happy. Happiness comes from within.

I was usually the one who emptied his dirty laundry bag upon his returning home from his trucking trips. One day, after he returned from a trip, I found pillowcases in his bag that I know did not belong to us. I had a feeling that he'd gotten a motel room because he found another woman to share it with him. His semi truck has a sleeper in it, but it's not big enough for two. I quickly dismissed those thoughts and suspicions because they were too painful to face. There were signs that he was still attracted to the old crowd and the drug world. He tried to impress them when we ran into them and he always wanted to stop and chat. I didn't. I thought we both had broken those ties completely but he didn't seem to want to let go. I ignored those signs too and I went on like nothing was wrong.

One Saturday afternoon, a year or so after my return from Cuba, Julio told me he wanted a divorce. I was taken aback. It wasn't a threat this time, it was a statement and I knew he meant it. I was so hurt. I felt used and stupid. I had brought back seven hours of videos of his family and children and grandchildren from Cuba, and now this?

Just before my trip to Cuba, Julio and I had quite a few arguments. I just wanted a little reassurance that everything would be okay, but he became frustrated. He yelled at me. "Do you think I'm sending you to hell? Do you think going to Cuba is like going to hell?" In an attempt to keep me from backing out, he played on my insecurities: "Remember, you wouldn't even have this kind of life if it wasn't for me."

He didn't give me credit for how far I had come. He accused me of not being grateful. I shrugged it off and told myself he didn't realize what he was saying. I actually felt selfish when I considered my fears and feelings about going to Cuba. Julio magnified those feelings by playing the guilt-trip game on me when I expressed my fears.

I went to Cuba for him, not me. I called it selfless and compassionate at the time but now I can see I was still navigating through life with the victim mindset. Just because I was traffic-free and drug-free didn't mean I no longer had issues. Going within and examining your own motives, on a daily basis is what recovery is all about. Becoming honest with yourself is what you have to do in order to live a life of total freedom.

The thought of divorce, at first, made me cringe. The thought of losing our beautiful home was devastating to me. I tried hard to change his mind, but as time went on, I simply could not overlook how he treated me.

Julio often instructed me on how I was to behave when we were around his family and friends. On our way back from a trip to his brother's house in Dallas, he let me know he disapproved of how I'd handled myself. He didn't want his family to view me as a big mouth. At the time, I questioned my behavior, and vowed to try harder.

Big mouth? What did I say? And to whom did I say it? He never explained specifically what I did wrong, and I didn't dare ask, so I didn't know what I had to do to "be better," but I blamed myself nonetheless.

Now that I look back, I can see that my husband was never concerned with how I might view his family. It was always the other way around. I tuned in to how I was actually feeling, which turned out to be exhausted and sick of working so hard to please him and to win his family over.

The transition from being a supportive husband to being so demeaning and uncaring was such a slow transition that I didn't notice it. I guess I kept the blinders on during most of our marriage because I didn't want to see it. The truth can hurt a lot.

When I finally faced that he didn't care for me, that maybe he never cared for me, that it was probably all a strategy on his part to keep me dedicated to him, I felt stupid and embarrassed. I felt dumb for allowing myself to, once again, get roped in by a man's charm. But the embarrassment didn't last long: I really *had* learned a thing or two. I realized that divorce was not that devastating to me after all.

Divorce was not going to make me hang my head in shame like my mother had. I had money, a car, and a job. I knew I'd never be homeless again, and I knew I'd never have to ask anyone for money ever again. I knew I'd never have to take crap from anyone to survive. I realized the divorce could be my ticket to freedom and independence.

We used only one lawyer, sold the house, split everything fifty/fifty, shook hands, and said goodbye. Before we parted, Julio made one last remark that reconfirmed his lack of respect for me: "I'm sure you'll end up back on the streets with the scum bags after the divorce." That remark was so uncalled for. I had begun to believe the reason he really wanted a divorce was because he just wanted to get back to his Cuban roots; that he just couldn't live away from his own culture any longer. I was feeling pretty much the same way. I wanted to get back to my roots too. But I could see he never respected me the way I needed to be respected. He thought I would go back to the streets? After being together for ten years, he really didn't know me. I proved him wrong.

Finally, at age forty-six and newly single, I realized that my judgment on the men I allowed in my life was seriously impaired and that never getting married again was the securest choice for me.

This quote from www.facebook.com/awesomequotes4eva resonates with me:

Some people will only "love you" as much as they can use you. Their loyalty ends where the benefits stop.

CHAPTER NINETEEN

The Mixed-Up Business Of Making Amends

I was forty-six. I had a secure job, money in the bank, I was debt-free, and my car was paid for. I figured I was in a good position to "give back." Who better to give back to, than my mother? She was eighty years old and I didn't feel comfortable with her living alone anymore.

When I took Mother in, my brother Ken got his life back. It was also my way of making amends to Mom for being such a bad daughter. I saw it as a win-win situation for all of us. I talked my siblings into allowing her to sell her house. I found a comfortable duplex for Mom and me to live in.

Unfortunately, my expectations were set too high—again. I thought she'd be so grateful that I took her in that we'd live "happily ever after," but Mother was still very verbally abusive.

My siblings knew that my decision to live with Mom was a bad move on my part, but for them it would be good because most of the burden of caring for our elderly mother would be on me.

I still expected mothering from her, and she still had unreasonable expectations of me. It was exhausting trying to manage her erratic and manipulative behavior. Living with her was a huge reminder of my childhood traumas. We bickered and argued. She grilled me about what I was doing, who I was doing it with, and why.

If she really felt remorse for treating me so badly when I was little, why is she still so verbally abusive now? Why did she even rescue me from that drug house to belittle me now?

Mom and I lived together for four years before I found a nice senior living place for her and I bought a small condo for me and my cat. She lived in her little apartment for six and a half years. I still tended to her, but not as much as before. I learned that I needed to put my own needs first, before I could reach out to others.

I'd been able to let go of the past abuse, but I couldn't deal with her present abuse. I knew I could spend a lifetime making amends to her for all I had put her through. I reasoned with myself that if she couldn't accept my attempt to make amends to her, I still had to go on with my life. I had done my part and I'm so thankful I had the opportunity to do it. I wouldn't have been able to live with myself if I didn't at least try.

Narcotics Anonymous taught me that I had to make a sincere attempt to make amends to others before I would be able to keep moving forward—I had done just that. What I couldn't do, I left up to God to handle. My counselor taught me that forgiveness is not a one-time event, but a daily practice. I was finding it to be difficult to practice on a daily basis.

Many times I would pick her up and take her with me while I ran errands, just to get her out of the house. She needed to use a walker and always looked forward to getting out of the house.

When I'd arrive, instead of acting pleased to see me, or greeting me with words of love, she would drill me. "Where have you been? I've been waiting and waiting. What did you have to do that was so important?"

There was a time when I came to Mother's apartment with a letter in my hand. In the letter I listed everything I needed an apology for. I was full of emotion as I handed her this list.

She said, "What is this?"

I said, "It's a letter from me to you. I just want to drop it off."

I didn't dare stick around to see her reaction. The list said I expected and deserved an apology for when she called me a whore after I told her I was raped, and for directing my life on a road of self- destruction, shame, disease, addiction, and being an outcast.

I didn't hear from her for two days. She ended up calling me and asked me to come over. When I arrived she didn't greet me with interrogating questions or ridicule. Her face was stern as she looked down at the floor.

I broke the ice. "Did you read my letter?"

She said, "Yes, I did."

I said, "Well?" I was shaking but I managed to hide this from her. I'd wanted to do this for so long.

It felt so good to write it down. After writing it, I played the scene out in my head and imagined how it would go if I gave it to her. I envisioned how good it would feel to hear her say she was sorry, to hear her acknowledge how her abuse affected my life.

As I stood with my hands on my hips, she said, "I know I probably treated you badly at times, Ruth, but your father was drunk all the time and I had the other kids to feed...and..."

My anger started to build when I heard the word "but." I interrupted her and repeated what she'd said, "You treated me badly *but*? What kind of an apology is that? I was just a kid and you weren't there for me! I never would have had syphilis if you would have protected me. I wouldn't have Hep C today if you would have been there for me!"

She was crying, and so was I.

I knew then there would no talking to her about this. I was just going to get angrier and angrier if I stayed, so I walked out and left her sitting in her chair crying. I jumped in my car and cried out loud as I drove home.

It crossed my mind that maybe she would have a heart attack and I second-guessed my decision to confront her. I thought maybe the best thing to do was just cross her off completely because we were so toxic for each other. I couldn't fathom continuing a relationship with her because I could no longer pretend nothing happened. I was sick of walking around the elephant in the room. Either we cleared the air or forgot *everything*.

Mother never verbally apologized to me for the crimes committed against me. An apology was certainly in order, after the abuse I suffered as a child, but I didn't want to be angry all the time. I didn't want to be so full of rage and confusion. But how can one forgive when there is no apology?

Even if she were sincerely remorseful, I'm sure Mother had no idea how to apologize, so I chose to see her rescuing me from the drug house as her apology to me—in actions, instead of in words. I still longed for the words. I still longed for her to acknowledge how the crimes against me affected my life. But she never did. A sincere, verbal apology would have saved me years of heartache and repaired our relationship long before she became old, but it never came.

I eventually learned not to scream right back at her. I learned to remain calm and assert myself without blowing up. "I'm going to carry on with my day without you and when you can talk to me with more respect, I'll be back." Then I would just leave. This way of responding to Mom felt so much better.

I finally figured out how to fend off her abusive treatment and she learned to be careful with her words because she knew I'd leave. After a while, we had good times.

For so long I'd been afraid of standing up to her, and to others. Because of my PTSD, I feared almost everything and many times I buckled at the knees, just thinking about standing up for myself. But Mother reacting to me differently as a result of my setting boundaries was proof that standing up for myself could open the door to healthier relationships. Setting boundaries teaches others how you want to be treated. People have to know how far they can go with you.

Love cannot exist without boundaries. Our relationship improved after I set boundaries with her. On warm days we'd sit on her front porch and put names to the shapes we thought the clouds were making and we'd laugh and laugh. There was a bike path near her apartment; I rode my bike to her apartment on nice summer days and together we would ride down the path, me on my bike and her on her Hoveround. I cherish the good times we had there.

She loved to come along when I went grocery shopping, just to sit in the parking lot and people-watch while I shopped. When I returned to my car, she always had funny stories about the action in the parking lot.

Our conversations never got deeper than that, though. I wanted to know more about her life, but she would never talk about it. I wanted to have heart-to-heart talks with her, but she just couldn't.

After living in the senior community for six and a half years, Mom had a massive stroke and was moved to a nursing home, at the age of ninety. She was in diapers and couldn't move her left side at all.

I decided to be there for her, with or without a verbal, sincere apology. The day Mother was admitted to the nursing home, I had strong flashbacks to the day she'd admitted me to Pine Rest. I thought of how she walked down the hallway and never looked back and left me there.

I knew the dark emotions of fear and loneliness after being left in a strange place to fend for myself. I didn't want to leave her there, but I had to. I was not going to let her fend for herself, though. She was the one who'd shown me that I was worth fighting, so I had to show her she was worth fighting for, too.

I'm sure she had her share of loneliness, abandonment, and abuse in her life—it was high time she knew that she had someone in her corner that was willing to fiercely fight for her and defend her.

Through my loving care for her, I hoped she would hear me tell her, "I forgive you."

Some people just can't accept love and affection from anyone. Mother was one of those people. With her, any communication about love and forgivingness had to be non-verbal. I looked beyond her behavior and did my best to manage her dysfunction. I lowered my expectations of her because I knew I had to be the stronger one. I turned to my inner guidance to meet my own needs and I became my mother's mother. I was doing all this for her—but also for me. I didn't want to live with regrets. Mother was a human being and a woman, just like me, so I had to do what I could for her. I shopped for her and took her out to the mall, or to the park. I advocated for her care with the staff. A handicap-equipped bus took her and her wheelchair around so she could spend many Sundays at my house and my sister's house. My siblings and I did what we could to keep her life as normal as possible in spite of her huge physical disability.

Once, after spending the day with her at the nursing home, I felt compelled to reassure her that she was not alone. I hesitated at the door and turned around to face her. I smiled and went back to her bedside. I held her hands and said, "Mother, I want you to know that I will never leave you."

She got so choked up. She tried so hard to hold back the

tears, but couldn't. She squeezed my hand and blurted, "Thank you." Her memory wasn't good anymore, so I often reminded her of my loyalty. I knew I'd want to be reassured, if I was in her shoes. I wanted to give her what I needed as a child and also what she needed as a child. I knew better than she did, so I acted accordingly, and prayed for God to do the rest.

One day, out of the blue, while I was straightening out her closet, she said, "You are such a joy." She'd never talked like that before. I think I may have been getting through to her.

On summer days, I looked forward to going to the nursing home to wheel Mother to the home's back yard where there was a lovely park. I'd bring a basket full of snacks and drinks and we would sit and watch the kids play and the people go by. Hours would go by and neither of us would say a word to each other; but we didn't have to. The non-verbal communication between us was clear: we simply enjoyed being together.

There is no doubt in my mind that Mother loved all of her kids. Deep down, she had a loyalty to us that kept her going. I'm convinced she was terribly abused during her childhood, and I know it continued during her marriage and motherhood.

Yes, I admit, Mother was "messed up." I'm pretty sure her mother was, too, and as you know, I was, too. When a child is abused, traumatized, and neglected, do you really expect them to grow up with no issues when their traumas are never addressed?

Mom navigated through her PTSD the best she could, just as I had. Others could see she was a mess, but people could see I was a mess, too; yet I was forgiven and given a second chance. She deserves forgiveness. My dad had the liberty to walk away and give up; Mother didn't.

My dad was a mess and a bad parent, too, but I can forgive him now. As we age, we reflect back on our lives and we come to regret some of our actions and decisions. My father could have made an attempt to rekindle a relationship with me, but he chose not to. My mother tried to, in her own disabled way, but my father moved on. I guess he was trapped by his demons and was just too scared to face them.

Everyone has to weigh the benefits and consequences of their own situations when forgiveness and compassion is concerned. There may be a time to forgive and a time of being not yet ready to forgive. Listen to your heart; let your inner guidance lead you.

Researching my family's history and studying PTSD helped me realize the cycle of abuse my family was trapped in, which ultimately led me to forgive. I looked at the big picture.

I visited my eighty-year-old aunt at the nursing home she was in and told her about the abuse my mother and us kids were subjected to. I wondered if maybe I shouldn't have mentioned it because she was so shocked. She and my mother were close for years. They were brought up together. She responded to the news by saying, "Oh-oh-oh! Now I know the truth! Oh-oh-oh!"

My mother had hidden the abuse from everyone, taking a lot of secrets with her to the grave. I can't imagine a life like that. I wish she were alive to experience the era I am blessed to live in today. Maybe she would have come out with her horror stories. If she'd had a trusted friend or counselor to unload on like I had, maybe her life would have been different. Back then I don't think it was common for even friends to admit domestic violence and/or rape to each other.

I can only imagine what it was like for my parents and the families of that era. In that era, many women and wives were raped and then shamed and shunned for it. Many boys and men were abused and then sent to war. How could they come to believe there was any place for love in this world? Now we know so much more about the effects of trauma and PTSD, so I foresee things to be better for the next generation. That is my prayer anyway.

I wanted to know more about Mom's childhood. How she met my father. How she came to place me in Pine Rest. How she gathered the strength to stand up to her abusive husband and then divorce him. How she held down five jobs at one time. How she came to put her life on the line for me and rescue me from the drug house. But it didn't matter after a while. We both experienced healing through forgiveness and acceptance, and we became the best of friends before she died.

Now that I look back, I can clearly see that Mother had so many issues of her own that she didn't know how to love others, not even her kids. She didn't have a clue what was "wrong with me." I was desperate for love. That's what was "wrong" with me, and that's probably what was "wrong" with her, too. Mother was a battered woman and a victim, herself.

I'm amazed at the strength mom mustered up to stand up to dad when she finally did it. She was forty-nine years old and had two teenage girls still at home when the divorce was granted. The stigma of divorce back then carried a lot of shame as did being a battered woman.

Before the no fault divorce laws were passed in 1973, the husband had absolute rights to physically discipline his wife. In 1966 beatings by the husband was deemed cruel and inhumane and became grounds for divorce in New York, but the plaintiff had to establish that a "sufficient" number of beatings had taken place.

These facts show me how and why a lot people in my parents' and grandparents' era must have had PTSD too.

Studies have shown that if traffickers can find the ones who were neglected and abused at home, they have half of their brainwashing work already done for them. Those who are repeatedly abuse can become easy prey for any predator. Repeated abuse can cause one to acquire the victim mindset. They get trapped believing there is no hope for escape. In my parents and grandparents era there truly was no escape for many because of the strict divorce laws and lack of laws that would allow women an alternative.

All during her time at the nursing home, I hoped and prayed that, through me, she would feel an unconditional love that she had forever longed for. I hope I gave her what she needed before she died.

On her deathbed, I held her hand when she said she couldn't see. I bent over to her ear and whispered, "Don't be afraid of the darkness, Mom. God wants to take you home." She squeezed my hand and twenty minutes later, she died. I felt a lot of peace that day.

My siblings and I have fun reminiscing about the good times today. When we were little, our parents rented cottages and we had a blast during our vacations there. When I look back, I think these vacations were stressful for Mom, though. Us kids had fun on the boat and exploring in the woods, but Mom was always tense and uptight; she didn't enjoy the amenities our vacations offered.

And then there were the big Dutch Sunday dinners, which continued into our adulthood. Mom prepared dinner for us after church every Sunday. She never missed going to church on Sunday, even after she was excommunicated for being a divorced woman.

I can't explain when or how this was but I do remember sitting on Mom's lap when I was little, maybe six or seven years old and she would sing me a song, "You are my sunshine, my only sunshine. You make me happy when skies are grey. You'll never know dear, how much I love you. Please don't take my sunshine away."

CHAPTER TWENTY

My Siblings And I Today

When I was little, I was afraid of my siblings, even though I subconsciously looked for parenting from them—and I continued that expectation into adulthood. I now know that I was asking too much from them. For a long time I believed they were "in the know" and were just refusing to clue me in on it. All six of us survived awful abuse and have had our struggles in life. We all carry a heavy load because of our childhoods.

But we see each other often. We have many good memories to reminisce about and many bad ones to still sort through. We've all learned a lot from our experiences and mistakes, and we're still learning as we go, just like everyone else.

A few years after I had escaped "the life," my siblings admitted to me that they knew where all my dysfunction stemmed from. They told me they knew I took the brunt of the abuse in our family, being the baby. It meant a lot to me to hear that. I guess that kind detective wasn't the only one who'd had a hunch that I didn't knowingly sign up for "the life" after all.

I also learned from my brother Ken that he'd enlisted in the army to escape the road he was on. Back then a lot of vets enlisted for the same reason. He was getting into trouble with the bad crowd he was hanging around with in the neighborhood. He said "they had crossed the line" as far as he was concerned regarding the trouble they were getting into, and he didn't want anything to do with it anymore, so he'd enlisted in the army. While in the army, he thought of the two little sisters he'd left behind and he feared for our safety; he wrote a letter to one of his buddies and warned him to stay away from us.

When I was forty-nine, I told Ken about the rapes when I was little. After comparing notes, we figured out that I was raped by the man he wrote the letter to.

Even after all these years, after I had put it all in the past, Ken still felt compelled to apologize to me for not being there for me. It meant a lot to me to hear that, but my heart went out to him, too. I can just imagine what it felt like to know your little sister had no protection after he went to war and that his letter didn't do any good.

Later in life my other siblings and I compared notes and we were all surprised to learn of the abuse that the others had suffered through as children.

The strong culture of shame in our era left my family without recourse. There were no resources for us as a family who lost a family member to human trafficking. It's amazing to me how my family persevered and how we all learned what love and respect is. We should all be so very proud.

CHAPTER TWENTY-ONE

Dear Ruthie, 1962

My counselors today advise me to write and journal to continue to heal myself. Writing letters is another way we can heal ourselves, even if the letter is never sent or read by anyone.

I know now that I unknowingly walked into the open arms of traffickers as a child. I know now that I was victimized. I know that, because of the fear that was inflicted in me, I had learned to settle for terrible treatment. Also, I can now see what it took for me to take the blinders off. Because of this, I'm able to accept my past for what it was. I don't deny my past anymore. It's a part of me. If I had been cherished and taught self worth in childhood, all of this mess could have been prevented.

When I realized that love was the missing link in my life, the one thing that could have prevented many years of turmoil, I wrote a loving letter to my eleven-year-old self.

I wrote the letter as if it was from someone who cared and could offer resources to my mother and me. It is my prayer that there will be resources for those like us now that society better understands human trafficking an the effects of trauma.

Dear Ruthie (of 1962):
I can only imagine how hard things must be for you. After what you have been through, I can only imagine how confused and alone you must feel.

I heard how a man tricked you into going with him when you were at the plaza, and how badly your mother reacted when you told her. Your mother reacted that way because she didn't know any better. I had a talk with your mother and she knows now that she was wrong, and she feels bad that she wasn't there for you. She wants to apologize to you for that. You are not tainted or damaged because of what happened and you certainly are not a whore, like she said. She wants to ask you if she can take her words back. You are a precious child, and anyone who makes you doubt that is wrong.

That man doesn't want anyone to know what he did that day because he knows he did wrong. You may think his secret is one you must keep in order to fend off being judged or humiliated, but, Ruthie, please know in your heart that you do not have to carry the shame of what happened to you. He committed a shameful act and he is the one who should be ashamed. He's hoping that you will feel so ashamed that you will keep his secret and not expose him. He is an adult who knows better; an adult who should be protecting young kids like you, not lying to them. He is the adult and you are just a child who is going to be confused by all this because you're still so young.

It is totally understandable why you went with him. You believed you were doing the right thing by doing what you were told. You trusted him, and he betrayed your trust. You did nothing wrong. He did. You may tell yourself we can't blame him, that he did nothing wrong because you went along with it, that he didn't use force, but you were violated just the same, my dear.

If you tell someone, who trusts you totally, to walk to the corner, knowing there is danger waiting for them on that corner, wouldn't you be putting them in danger yourself, even though they're the one who walked there? Yes. If we know there is danger on the corner, and we lead them to the corner anyway, we are wrong: we are guilty of putting them in harm's way and guilty of tricking them into walking into danger. This is what happened to you. This man knew he was leading you into danger but he did it anyway.

I know your family fights a lot and you may not feel you can turn to them when you're in need. I am so sorry your family and home feel so unpredictable and so unsafe for you.

It's totally understandable that you may feel lost and alone at this point. How does a precious child find a way to preserve a sense of trust in people when her own mother betrays her? How can she feel safe in a house that sees violence as normal? How does she gain a sense of control in a situation that is terrifyingly unpredictable? How does she gain power in a situation that seems so helpless?

There is a way, Ruth. You can gain a sense of control over yourself and you can trust some people. You are a lovable child and there are people who want to love and protect you, who want to teach you how to keep yourself safe and teach you how to recognize it when someone is tricking you into doing something you feel uncomfortable doing. There are loving people out there you can trust. Not everyone is like that creepy man at the plaza. There are people who can teach your mother to handle this better than she did too.

Because this happened to you, you should talk about it to someone who can help make sense of it. Life can be complicated and confusing, but you can learn to sort through the confusion with help from people who know how. There are adults who went through this same thing when they were little; they grew up and learned that it's not their fault. Now they can help you make sense of all this.

I am here for you if you want to talk about it. I don't want you to feel so alone.

Sincerely,

Someone who cares.

CHAPTER TWENTY-TWO

The Anti-Human Trafficking Movement

I hope that, after reading my story, you realize that shame causes havoc and chaos in our lives.

Predators target those with obvious vulnerabilities, those who don't know any better, the naïve, those who carry a lot of shame.

Women who were raped as children are at a very high risk of entering a life of trafficking and addiction because rape is shaming, and shame is a self-worth injury. Rape can result in the victim mindset, and life is not compassionate to the victim mindset. It can put you on a dark and lonely path of self-destruction.

I've been to many anti-human trafficking events and conferences since I've been in the Anti-Human Trafficking Movement. I have learned so much more about me and about human trafficking, but human trafficking is a new field.

There are a lot of well-intentioned folks in this movement and if it weren't for some of them, I wouldn't have found my voice, but there is also a lot of wrong information being given on this topic and, human trafficking is getting sensationalized. It's sad but I think it's to be expected. Anything to do with sex is always sensationalized. That's our culture. We still have a long way to go.

We need to come back down to earth about these subjects. Humans are sexual beings and we need to address sex topics as natural, because it *is* natural. We are too quick to hone in on another's shame and sex is an easy tool to use to create scandal.

Adults feel more uncomfortable when talking about sex than our kids do. Child Protection Training classes can assist adults with how to initiate these conversations with our kids. Kids have a lot of questions about sex. We need to answer their questions at a young age before they get older and learn to feel ashamed and embarrassed by it. They need to feel free enough to ask their parents or a trusted adult their questions. Our kids learning about sex for the first time from somewhere else should scare all of us. We pass our shame on to our kids unknowingly. If we are too embarrassed to talk intelligently to our kids about sex, they will feel too embarrassed to talk about it too. We need to demonstrate to our kids what an intelligent conversation looks like and how it is supposed to go. (See websites and resource page).

When we can shift away from the shame of sex and the sensationalism of HT, we will then be able to have good conversations around it. Without intelligent conversation around it we will continue to send and receive the wrong messages. You can't scare or shame anyone into learning. There is too much focus on fear in HT right now and it can be too emotionally draining for the participant to retain the information being given. Let's face it HT is a dark subject. We want to look the other way because it IS so dark so if we focus too much on the darkness and fear in training programs, we are only giving the participant another reason to look the other way. Parents, health care workers, advocates, counselors, social workers and law enforcement already have enough drama to deal with in their work. (See description page HUMANTRAF-FICKINGELEARNING.COM)

DO SEX WORKERS REALLY HAVE A CHOICE?

You have to know what goes on behind closed doors to be able to answer that question because it can all look normal on the outside, but behind closed doors it can be obvious. It also depends on if one is being totally honest with themselves and others or not because a victim can be abused and settle for it, thinking it's normal.

This question brings me back to when I was 12 years old. The rapist told me he could tell I enjoyed it. Because he was adult and I was just a child I saw him as more credible than me. I didn't even know a crime was being committed against me so I reasoned with myself that because he was gentler with me than the first rapist was, I was supposed to enjoy it. I figured because he's an adult, he knows more about this than I do.

I took this confusion with me into adulthood. I thought everybody was "in-the-know" except me. After I was gang raped by those four men I heard one say, when it was over, "She really got into it." I know now that their plan was to keep me confused and it worked.

In adulthood I want to do what I am supposed to do too; but for a long time I denied my own feelings for the sake of doing what others thought I was supposed to do. I allowed another to determine my own beliefs and feelings. When I became honest with myself I just couldn't deny myself anymore. Today I know what I like and what I don't like. I know what I enjoy and what I don't enjoy. I refuse to be confused on this any longer. I can say yes and no when I want to. No one else will ever determine that for me again. This IS the land of the free.

How can anyone enjoy being raped every day? How can anyone enjoy performing sexually every day with multiple partners? In order for sex to be the beautiful thing it is meant to be, there has to be an inner connection between the two partners and also very good communication. How can there be an inner connection with multiple partners, everyday? How can sex be beautiful when the communication is always only superficial? I think it should be called the rape trade.

I believe that the more money and power imbalance in any relationship, the more dangerous it can become, and the better the chances of getting trapped or of trapping someone. Living a simple life equals peace to me.

Anyone who seeks out children or adults for the purpose of buying sex is not thinking of making love to them. They don't care about them, their welfare or their future. They only have deviant and/or violent sex acts in mind. Human trafficking victims never know what the next customer will do once they are alone with them and the door is closed. HT victims put themselves in positions of sheer powerlessness every day. There has to be something or someone behind it for them to continue in this life. The key to true freedom is when we are honest with ourselves.

Law enforcement has the daunting task of trying to decipher who should be deemed the victim and who should be deemed the suspect. Victims can become predators and predators may very have been victimized before. There are obvious situations, when it's clear who the victim is and who the predator is but when you peel back the layers and hear some of the stories there can also be a fine line.

If an HT victim victimizes and/or preys on and/or trafficks the vulnerable themselves, then we have both a victim and a predator. Law makers have to be specific in the laws they pass because victims can be treated unfairly and predators can get off scot free. Unfortunately, many times it's not clear to law enforcement how to handle these situations. Of course the victims have to come forward and many times this doesn't happen. I believe in justice for all but HT situations are not always black and white and the laws aren't always that clear either.

One law that IS clear is that children who fall prey to pedophiles or traffickers are clearly victims of rape and human trafficking. No evidence of coercion or force has to be presented for minors to be legally deemed as victims. Without HT training for law enforcement, however, victims will continue to fall through the cracks. The federal government deems them as victims but the state and local government need to get their laws in place to follow suit.

HOPING FOR CHANGE

It is so sad that many children hear loving and understanding sentiments for the first time from their future pimps. We must remember that children cannot consent to sex under any circumstance. They are child victims and survivors of rape. They cannot weigh the benefits and consequences because they are too young and naïve on the subject. They grow up never being able to see how sex could ever be beautiful like it's meant to be.

It's impossible to spot a victim of human trafficking by looking at them. Many never would have guessed in a million years that I was being trafficked. Only those closest to me would have been able to recognize the dysfunction, but of course the dysfunction was deemed as only an addiction problem back then. No one connected it to Human Trafficking or child abuse because it just wasn't talked about back then.

If you notice any of your children with clothes that you did not buy for them, look into it. Maybe the wrong person is spending money on them. If your children are associating with an older group of people, look into it. This may be a sign of sex trafficking. If you find your daughters are being promiscuous, look into it; promiscuity can be a sex trafficking sign. If your daughter's boyfriend doesn't have a job, simply don't trust him. Keep your eyes and ears open.

Most women who are trafficked have felony arrests, either for prostitution or for drug offenses. They don't have a regular address, but sleep in a variety of drug houses or at johns' houses. They often do not receive regular medical care. They are beaten by their pimps, and often by johns, too. They can experience numerous miscarriages and/or forced abortions. From the miscarriages, abortions, and diseases, and from all the abuse their bodies endured, many are unable to conceive anymore.

Pimps offer their victims a glamorous life. There are parties, and money, and nice clothes, and the thrill of getting high, but it's not like the money a trafficked girl makes goes into her 401K. The money made only fuels the cycle of drug addiction, fear, and violence. Not glamorous, at all.

Until recently, prostitution-related laws protected the pimps and criminals involved in the sex trade. Trafficked women were not considered victims and even children were arrested for prostitution.

Thankfully, this is changing. Now, trafficked women are considered victims by federal law and many state and local law enforcement agencies. More police attention is directed towards the pimps and the johns. Now, law enforcement conducts investigations to see who is behind it when an arrest of soliciting or prostitution is made.

This was a huge victory for me and for many others who were coerced or forced into the sex trade. Public awareness is improving, myths are being challenged, and survivors are finding better help than in the past, just like survivors of domestic violence found help when the public awareness was pushed and the stigma of divorce was challenged. My mother was empowered when the laws against domestic violence were passed. The term "battered women" was still not a part of the public's vocabulary in 1974.

I have hope for the next generation because I believe the human trafficking laws that are being passed to protect victims in many states will empower them to be able to resist the brainwashing techniques that traffickers use.

The stigma of commercial sexual exploitation is still strong—both the social stigma and the personal fear and shame. Because there were no child protection measures set into place when I was little, many fell prey to traffickers, as I did. They grew up to know the stigma all too well, but I foresee that the statistics of those falling prey in the next generation will be minimal.

By the time I'm old and gone, I pray we will be a nation that knows the signs and that will intervene to prevent our children, and the children around the world, from having to grow up living in the margins of society.

CHAPTER TWENTY-THREE

What To Do About Shame, Fear, And Mistrust

Not talking about our shame only feeds the demon of shame and compounds the effects it has on our lives; and silence protects the perpetrators. For those who already have low self-esteem and already feel they only deserve pain or suffering, like I did, rape validates that feeling. I was not allowed to talk about that first rape, when I was eleven, so I didn't talk about the others. In fact, because of the fear, shame, and mistrust the rapes had instilled in me, when I had the chance to talk, I couldn't. The pain of rape doesn't stop once the rape is over—not even close.

Dr. Brene Brown says, "When we tell our stories or share an experience with someone and they respond with empathy, most of our shame loses its power."

My friends, my counselors, and my sisters were there for me. They talked with me and they listened as I went on and on. They validated my fears and feelings. They let me cry it out. I thank God for them. Without them, I may very well have committed suicide.

They were able to empathize with me, which is not easy for a lot of people to do. Many people enjoy blaming and putting others down. For some, all they know to do when they hear another's shame story is to point fingers. I am so blessed for everyone in my life who did not blame me. I never would have been able to escape the life of slavery without them; I never would have become healthy enough or strong enough to write this book.

Many people have asked the same questions and made the same comments after attending my anti-human trafficking presentations. Hearing their questions and comments made me more aware of how empathy does not come naturally to any of us. I have learned not to take many comments personally because I know empathy is a skill that has to be acquired.

Victims can end up taking others' lack of empathy personally, and then they regret opening up at all, and often relapse back into silence. This is why victims should only unload with a trauma informed professional or another survivor who has been there, done that.

I don't think non-survivors, even some professionals, like social workers, medical professionals and law enforcement officers can easily understand what they are asking of a survivor when they ask them to tell their stories or recount their traumas. Also, I can see that some don't understand what survivors need from them to help them tell their story. Training is necessary for them too. I would like to address both the advocate and the victims/survivors to help them work together.

When victims of HT are being interviewed or assessed, understanding what you are really asking them to do will help you avoid pitfalls and avoid stumping the recovery process for the victim.

Remember, victims of HT carry a lot of shame. What you are really asking them to do is show you their shame. No one is going to be quick to do this.

I'm sure we all know what shame feels like but HT victims carry a much heavier load of shame that no one person can carry alone.

What victims have to do is go down a dark, deep and bottomless hole to retrieve that shame. They won't be willing to do this if they feel you will only shame them even more. They have to know your intentions are genuine, because to them, the devil is in that hole waiting for them, hoping they will fall.

You can help them feel safe by giving them a rope to hang onto while you hold on tight to the other end at the top. Once they're down in the hole, they will look up at you for reassurance that you won't let go of your end. When they can see you are hanging on tight, they will then be able to draw from your strength and retrieve their shame.

Then you will have to pull them back up to the top, because they will be weak. Remember, this shame is very heavy. Once they are at the top and realize they are on solid ground, they will feel safer around you and more willing to open up. When they do open up, be ready, because there will be a lot that needs to be unloaded. This is how victims can transform to victors.

I want to add a caution here. Once they start to open up, please be careful because they may be willing to unload it all on you and you may find their dark stories too hard to bear. The unloading moments needs to be done with a trauma-informed professional or with one who is experienced in this kind of a thing. It's important that you don't excuse yourself from the room during the moment of unloading and don't interrupt them because they can feel like you are pushing them back down the bottomless hole.

You can take one step forward but two steps back if the unloading moments are not handled with care. They need a listening ear. It's important for law enforcement officers and healthcare workers to have a protocol in place for a forensic nurse or an experienced professional to be available for the unloading.

It took years for me to get to this point of telling my story to groups and writing this book—it's a long process.

If we don't know how to empathize we act with only our good intentions. I understand it may be difficult to empathize with human trafficking victims, but it's important that all of our words and actions come from love for the other person, from goodness and kindness, or else we can end up talking down to them, lecturing them. If you don't know how to respond after hearing their dark story, it's best to admit that and say, "I just don't know what to say right now, but I'm so glad you told me." If you patiently listen to them, they will be able to draw from your strength.

Be careful when you offer solutions. When we offer a seemingly simple solution to huge issues, victims can feel you are minimizing their ordeal or discounting what they are saying. You have to use good judgment about when to offer solutions, how you offer them, and what you offer. The homeless people you see on the street don't appreciate it when you offer them prayer instead of food when they are obviously hungry. They can feel insulted if you offer a seemingly simple solution when it's so obvious their needs are so huge. An offer of help can become *coercion to giving a confessional* if not handled correctly. They can feel shamed even further by your tactics if you're not well trained and equipped to avoid these pitfalls.

Empowering victims to become their own best friends is the key. The role of the advocate is to empower victims so they are able to articulate what happened to them, and also so they can use their own abilities to problem-solve and come up with their own solutions to get out of their situations and on their own feet. Being able to problem-solve will come easier to them once they have unloaded, but remember that they may have a lot to unload. Oppression keeps one from expressing emotions; over time, emotions get built up inside and victims may have a lot of catching up to do.

In the meantime, they need free housing. They need help with safety issues, financial, employment or education issues, and also their medical issues. No one can deal with their emotional health when they have to stay focused on survival needs.

I want all advocates to know how important it is that you don't take anything personally. If you do, it can keep you from focusing on the needs of the victims. It can also put a wedge in communication and in the recovery process for the victim.

Be careful when you express your love or compassion to the victim. Saying, "I love you," can be taken the wrong way. I heard police officers telling a teen victim that she was a princess, and later they said, "We love you." I know their hearts may very well have been in the right place, but if I would have heard that from a police officer while he was trying to "rescue" me, I would have taken it like I could count on him the next time I fell, too. Victims can become too clingy when people reach out to them, so while being compassionate, you have to practice detachment at the same time. You don't want them to become dependent on you or anybody. It takes a team to hold them up. If only one person is holding them up, they will become too reliant on that one person and won't learn to problem-solve on their own and build a circle of supporters.

The only way many victims know how to deal with strong feelings is by being rude or belligerent, or acting out. Don't take this personally, either. Remember, you may very well have said something that triggered a traumatic stress response in them, but it's their past that is causing these strong emotions.

People, places, and things can trigger memories in all of us, but for those who suffer from PTSD, it's the memory of their past traumas that they are having a hard time with, not you. They would be triggered whether you crossed their path or not. They need you to understand this or the healing process can be stumped.

When I looked back it's hard to believe that I was that

confused. Words of hope on the walls were helpful for me. They caused me to reflect on my situation and consider a different perspective.

It was helpful to hear my counselor tell me that he too had the same feelings I had before. It made me feel I am just as human as the next person. It lifted me up a notch and I saw myself on the same level as him.

One counselor told me a personal story of how he overcame stuttering. That was huge for me. It made me realize that I wasn't the only one with embarrassing secrets.

I had spent a lifetime of trying to manage others' emotions instead of my own. It took a long time to get acquainted with myself but through counseling I am finally able to tune into to my own emotions.

Victims and survivors: PLEASE BE CAREFUL WHO YOU SPILL YOUR GUTS TO. Consider whether you are strong enough to handle it if the person you are telling cannot empathize. You have to learn how to listen to that voice inside you. Test the waters. No one knows what's best for you better than you.

Don't trust blindly. Give others bits and pieces of you at first and take it slow. Listen to that voice inside you when considering giving of yourself in any given situation. Remember what happened when you trusted blindly in the past. Even those with titles, like your counselor, may not have good intentions. Even if their intentions are good, they may not be able to empathize, so don't ignore your gut feelings. You don't want to leave yourself open to being exploited all over again. If you feel uncomfortable or afraid, remember you are feeling that way for a reason. It's a message you need to pay attention to.

Hollywood glorifies pimps and hos. We tend to be desensitized to the message they give. You can even buy a pimp or a hoe costume for Halloween. There's something wrong with this picture.

At this time there isn't enough data on human trafficking available for the statistics to be accurate but some of the statistic seem very accurate to me. It is estimated that child sexual abuse makes up 40% of all human trafficking cases, and 70% to 90% of all trafficked women were sexually abused as children. I'm apt to believe these estimates are quite accurate. Many of the women I was on the street with have very similar childhoods.

CHAPTER TWENTY-FOUR

My PTSD

Please remember, we are victims, not criminals. We didn't choose to be enslaved or abused. We walked into it not knowing what we were in for. Traffickers know how to entrap victims psychologically; they are very clever psychopaths. The stigma that keeps victims in their place is the belief that they are not capable of being victimized, but we are all capable of being victimized.

Life is good for me now. My past will always be there. It still comes back to me in unexpected ways; these are called PTSD triggers. I handle these triggers so much better today than I did in the past. Most of the time I call these triggers "reminders." Now, when I reflect on my past, I'm reminded of how blessed I am today.

Now I can make sense of my past. I know now that it was shame that drove me into the arms of traffickers and it's only by the grace of God that I'm alive today—the power of forgiveness lifted me out of that life.

Even years after I escaped "the life" there were still people, places, and things that triggered my PTSD. I would run into my therapist's office many times, after requesting an extra long lunch hour at work because of a panic attack I was having. I greeted my therapist with, "Look, I'm in trouble and you can't tell me it's in my head either!" Nothing riled her up. Her calming presence was exactly what I needed. She'd let me unload on her once again and I'd go back to work ready to take on the afternoon. I panicked because I was convinced my life was ruined after being recognized by someone from my past. I worked in customer service. My thoughts went from A to Z (calm to paranoid) after I waited on this person on the job.

It was high anxiety for me at work every day because of my thoughts and fears. Yes, I had good days, along with the bad days and I remained professional in all my duties. The closer I got to retirement the more I believed I'd made it and no one could target me or take me down anymore. I made it to retirement and now I am free to speak the truth and allow myself to be seen. I'm so grateful. Now I find myself mimicking my therapist when I'm with someone who is stressed out or having a panic attack. I know how remaining calm can affect them. Remaining calm can be contagious.

I relived the terror of the rape in the apple orchard and of the man with the switchblade many times over. I would gaze out the passenger window while traveling on a highway at night, passing a wooded area, an orchard, or an open field and I would see myself running through them, trying to find my way out; my heart would race and I would silently cry. Oftentimes the driver would ask me what was wrong. I couldn't explain it. I tried hard to hide that I was in turmoil because I didn't want to appear crazy or distraught.

I was reluctant to fall asleep because of frequent nightmares. But as the years went by, and after many sessions with therapists and counselors, the nightmares subsided. I still have bad dreams at times, but when I wake up, I know that I'm safe and I can easily go back to sleep.

If my PTSD was so debilitating for me, can you imagine what our soldiers go through, even long after the war is over?

Because my therapist allowed me to unload all my traumas on her, now I can even ride by apple orchards without my heart racing and without getting distraught. Today, apple orchards remind me of how fortunate I am to be alive. It is so true that facing your fears robs them of their power over you.

We *can* heal from traumas. Humans are resilient. But, they will always be in our memories. Now every New Year's Eve, especially if I'm at home, snuggled up with my cat, and its cold outside, I think back to the New Year's Eve when I was standing on a corner in a storm, and was confronted with a switchblade; I can't help but realize how blessed I really am.

One of my favorite ways to remain positive is to print out a list of my favorite affirmations, cut them out, and then fold them up small enough to put a handful of them in my pocket. Throughout my day, I open one up and read it. It's a great way to fill my mind with positive thoughts when my mind wanders off with negative ones.

In order to create more of what I want for my life, and eliminate what I don't want, I must become fully aware of what is going on in my thought world. Keeping an emotional balance and staying in the middle keeps me calm and able to make wise choices and decisions. Being too passive allows room for others to walk on me; being too aggressive allows room for conflict. Staying in the middle somewhere allows me to stay at peace with myself and with others.

I'm not proud of what I'm guilty of. I did some pretty stupid stuff, and made some really stupid choices. I hurt a lot of people and caused a lot of my own misery. I'll be making amends for the rest of my life, but I don't mind. I love to pay it forward and give back.

Living with a deep sense of pride is the only way to live. It is so wonderful to be able to walk with my head up. This is what I call living! Now, when I look into the mirror, I like the woman who is looking back at me. I am so proud of myself. I did well.

I used to compare myself to others, which resulted in depression. Now I compare my present to my past, which results in one thankful person. I have the opportunity to turn all the ugly into something positive, so how can I regret my past?

If others want to point a finger at me, accuse me, or discredit me, I will tell them:

"YOU DON'T KNOW WHAT I'VE BEEN THROUGH! YOU DON'T KNOW WHAT I HAVE OVERCOME! YOU DON'T KNOW THE WHOLE STORY. YOU ARE IN NO POSITION TO JUDGE ME."

CHAPTER TWENTY-FIVE

A Note On Enabling

I want to make a note about enabling. So far I've talked about how love, forgiveness, and understanding can be the key in preventing and in helping someone heal from PTSD, but I also want to mention that this approach may not always be the right one to use when reaching out to victims of HT who are addicted or alcoholics.

PTSD is not an excuse for abusing drugs or alcohol. PTSD can be managed without resorting to substance abuse. Addressing PTSD with love and forgiveness can be the key in fending off drug addiction, but when someone with PTSD resorts to abusing drugs to deal with it, it's a whole new ball game.

I believe love will always win, but loving an addict must be done strategically. Using "love" and "strategy" in the same sentence may seem conflicting, but loving an addict in the way you are accustomed to loving him or her, can enable him or her to continue their addiction and hinder or prolong recovery.

After years of abuse and of being addicted, I became a master manipulator, myself. My siblings can attest to the hell I put them all through. I feel the need to warn mothers and families about how easy it is to get caught up in the chaos of an addict's emergencies.

Drug addicts so easily get the wrong message when you help them by fixing their messes or loaning them money. To really help them, you need to stand in the way of them continuing their addiction. You must never contribute to their addiction.

Recognizing when you are contributing to their addiction is the kicker: you cannot continue to love them in the same way you did in the past. As a former drug addict myself, I see families and mothers of drug-addicted loved ones taken down because of the addict's destructive behavior.

My mother abused me, and later in life she enabled me. In her mind, the abuse wasn't abuse. She thought she was teaching me. She was never taught how to recognize enabling as enabling, either. It was just ignorance.

Guilt and shame can blind you from seeing what is right in front of you. I think my mother's guilt got heavier and heavier as the years went by. During my addiction she gave me money to help lessen the pain of her guilt. Guilt kept her from seeing that in reality she was contributing to my addiction and life of self-destruction.

Of course, she may have believed she was helping me eliminate the need to beg men, too. It's an awful position for a mother to be in; that's why mothers cannot do it alone. Letting go of your adult, addicted child is a task no mother can endure alone. It's so hard to watch your child walk down a dark and lonely path of self-destruction, knowing there's nothing you can do about it. I believe it's one of the most extreme heartaches that any mother could ever experience. When trying to manage an addict's manipulation and erratic behavior, you have to keep a balance. It can be so hard to do alone. You need support from others.

Realizing the addict's perspective can help mothers fend off being taken down themselves by their addicted child's destructive behavior. They need supportive people, like the people at Al-Anon, or another addict who has accomplished advanced levels of recovery and who can help them keep their eyes open to the manipulations they are being subjected to.

I have heard many mothers of addicted adult children say, "Looking back, I regret my naivety." Mothers of addicted adult children need to live by the same principles they want their children to live by, and that means setting boundaries, demonstrating what courage is, and demonstrating what "standing on your truth" is.

Loving an addict and protecting yourself at the same time can be a balancing act, so you have to stay focused on the message you're giving. The message you need to give them is: "I love *you*, but I despise the behavior."

Getting that message across to them can be the hardest thing for a mother to do. By nature, parents extend love and guidance to their children and many will take a bullet for them and are willing to take their place so they can be spared pain. Many loan them money and try to clean up their messes for them. When they are adults though, this kind of love and mothering can hinder their growth.

Addicts, many times, will blame others and the rest of world for their mess. Many need to hit rock bottom before they will take a hard look at who is really responsible for their mess. They need to understand how they got in their mess and why. They may have to hit rock bottom over and over before they will be willing to wave their white flag in surrender, like I had to.

When they have depleted all their resources, have lost all family and friends, and find themselves up against a wall, then, and only then, will they ask for help and be willing to try something new. They have to want change above all else and want it so bad that no one will stand in their way. If and when they ask for help, the help needs to be available to them. Many parents can help them, but there needs to be a professional involved, too.

Many addicts have anger issues and they need to identify where their anger comes from. A period of time must be spent on examining the boundary violations of the past that they never realized existed. Once the violations are realized they may have to do some catching up with that anger. They will need a safe place to get their anger out and that's what counseling is for.

After examining the particular violations, they may come to realize that it was actually the mistakes their parents made in raising them that turned their life for the worse. Be ready for this. Stay open to receive it and learn from it. Be ready to apologize for the mistakes you made. No parent is perfect. There is something that every parent can apologize for. You will also need to acknowledge how your mistakes affected their life, an apology won't be enough.

The addict must also own up to how they hurt others. It takes hard work and total honesty to reach this point but when you do, it will be so worth it. This is when true, heartfelt apologies can be granted to each other. Forgive and then move on, and keep the line of communication open.

Your love, support *and forgiveness* can be an important key to opening doors to their recovery and to help maintain their recovery.

I have a dear friend who helps me stay on track and helps me fend off the A-to-Z thinking of PTSD. I help her stay on track with her adult, addicted son. She wants to mother him and has a tendency to close her eyes to his dysfunction because she wants to believe in him so badly; but this, at times, enables him to remain addicted. I clue her in on the perspective of a drug addict to keep her eyes open.

To help an addict recover you need to learn about co-dependency, and you need to practice tough love.

When I finally realized that my brothers and sisters had convinced mother that she needed to let me go, that's when I looked for other resources to meet my needs and I left mother alone. I stopped hounding her. I knew I couldn't count on her or my siblings so I let them be. I knew it was over and I knew I was on my own. After being on my own and hitting many rock bottoms, I realized how badly I needed them. Then, and only then, was I willing to consider that my way was not working.

CHANGED

I am just a child, why is everyone so critical?
I'm being treated like I'm a criminal.
Can anybody hear me? Is anybody listening?
Please explain to me what is happening.
No one is interested; I'm all on my own
I still have questions, but now I'm grown
I'm being held responsible for what I was taught.
I'm just trying to survive, but that's not what they thought
The stigma and stereotype kept me in my place.
To society I was a disgrace
Is there any hope for me? What will I become?
I'm such a bad person; I'll just become a bum.
Ruth, who do you see when you look in the mirror?
I can't see me, the image is a blur
What are your interests? What is your grievance?
I can learn what they are; I just need a little guidance.
I don't know what you've been through
But I can see you lost your self value
I think you simply lost your way in life
But my dear, you CAN live a life free from strife
Making mistakes, doesn't make us immoral
What are you saying? You think I'm normal?
Yes, my dear; you are not the only sinner
You are only human and there are other attributes to consider.
I never heard anyone say that before. So many others said I was a
    whore.
This is great news that I thank you for telling
I rose up that day from a dark, lonely dwelling.
I can do something with my life after all
Now I'm determined that up from the bottom I will crawl.

162

I know the power and strength I hold within me
I will never again have to feel so empty
I am forgiven and now I can forgive
Helping others is now my motive
Even my battle with labels is over and done
I never knew life could be so much fun
Getting to know me is a work in progress
I can relax, just who am I trying to impress?
Because of Him my life was rearranged
I love my life.
THANK GOD I'M CHANGED!

Websites And Resources

CHILD PROTECTION TRAINING AND RESOURCES:

www.d2l.org

http://nationalchildrensalliance.org/

www.educatingthewholechild.org

Psychology Today, "Human Trafficking in America,"
by Dale Archer:
https://www.psychologytoday.com/blog/reading-between-the-headlines/201304/human-trafficking-in-america

https://www.youtube.com/watch?v=2rpfd_H4euU&feature=youtu.be

https://www.psychologytoday.com/blog/moral-landscapes/201412/why-kids-should-be-protected-toxic-stress

http://www.torontoaddictioncounselling.com/is-it-possible-to-put-trauma-into-words/

http://kirwaninstitute.osu.edu/wp-content/uploads/2015/06/2014_FCC_Report_140620.pdf

CHILDHOOD SEXUAL TRAUMA RESOURCES:

Healing from childhood sexual abuse, by Claudia Black,Ph.D.:
https://www.youtube.com/watch?v=fMFh0EDyG48

http://atzum.org/2012/12/03/prostitution-in-israel-myth-vs-reality/

PTSD:

60 Minutes Advanced PTSD Therapy (Vets & rape victims): https://www.youtube.com/watch?v=7frOWBiU8D4

END CHILD TRAFFICKING

www.thistlefarms.org www.thehealingplace.info

SHAME:

Shame and vulnerability researcher Dr. Brené Brown is amazing: https://www.youtube.com/watch?v=kAk4cwjvJ0A

The Courage to Heal by Ellen Bass and Laura Davis

Good read on how to set boundaries; undoing the victim mindset: *BOUNDARIES: WHEN TO SAY YES, HOW TO SAY NO* By Dr. Henry Cloud & Dr. John Townsend

HT TRAINING:

Online Training for Healthcare workers www.humantraffickingelearning.com

EFFECTIVE AFFIRMATIONS:

101 Ways to Transform Your Life by Dr. Wayne Dyer

The List of Human Bill of Rights resonated with me during the early stages of my reovery (and I go back to them often today): www.pete-walker.com/humanBillofRights.htm

Epilogue

In the process of writing my book, I was appointed by Governor Snyder to the MICHIGAN HUMAN TRAF-FICKING HEALTH ADVISORY BOARD in March of 2015. It is such an honor to serve on this board. I am still learning so much about myself, as well as about human trafficking and our government. I am so thrilled to be a part of it.

I am also co-authoring an online training program on HT for healthcare workers. (See websites and resources.) My co-author Patti Hathaway and I have the kind a relationship that is perfect for creating this kind of training. We can talk about the dark realities of HT because of her expertise in education and communication and my experiences of HT. It's rare to find a survivor and non-survivor who can communicate well enough to create a training program like this. I am blessed to have had the opportunity to know her and work with her. She has guided me along with invaluable advice as I walk in my anti-human trafficking journey that I will forever be thankful for. She is the daughter of Ken and Betty Navis. Ken is the counselor who helped me release the shame when I was 34 years old.

After I wrote this book, I passed it on to friends and family so I could get their feedback. Many asked, "Why, after so many years, did you decide to bring it all back up again?"

My response is, "Back up? How can anyone bring something back up when it was never laid to rest?" Child abuse, sexual abuse, and trafficking damaged me in every aspect of my life and destroyed everything of value in my life. I examined my motives over and over myself and the bottom line is that I needed to stop denying my past. Everything I don't deal with will continue to eat away at me; that's why I brought it all up again.

Writing it down in chronological order and trying to put it into a "nice and neat package" made me realize that my memory was failing me on the time frame of some events, and on the ages of some of the people I wrote about. Because I wanted to finish my book and because I wanted to be as accurate as possible, I had to research the facts in my past, so I searched public records. Knowing those dates and ages were key components in my healing process.

Victims don't realize that reliving their past without a professional, over and over, is what's holding them back. One sure way to bury your future is to keep digging up the past—but in order to keep the future in sight you need to keep your past in perspective *on a daily basis*. Because I have PTSD my past comes back to me in unexpected ways. Talking about my past helps me deal with it because it reminds me both of what it *was* like, and of what I'm blessed with today. No matter how far I go in life I will always remember where I came from. My past is what made me the person I am today. Going back to my past keeps me grateful and humble now that I've made progress in keeping it in perspective.

Now that I'm in the Anti-Human Trafficking movement, some ask me, "Why do you keep talking about it if you laid it to rest?"

My response is: Writing this book helped me to lay it to rest, get it out of my system, and move on. But there is no way out for me. It's a part of me. It's my life. Now that Human Trafficking is a phrase people can say it in public. How can I keep hiding my past, especially now? How can I just be quiet now that there is a movement? I would feel like a hypocrite all over again if I didn't speak up, if I didn't stay active in the movement. Child abuse and trafficking took eighteen years out of my life! I didn't choose that. I feel I have no choice now either.

I have lost friends because of my openness. Many don't understand and they simply don't want to hear it. Granted, HT may remind them of their own issues that they don't want to think about; I can understand that. I need to be sensitive to how human trafficking can evoke personal emotions and memories in others. I know how hard it can be to be around people who constantly remind you of things you don't want to be reminded of—but fighting human trafficking is what I do now. I have to surround myself with my supporters to be in this work.

The public conversation about human trafficking started just before I retired. There were commercials on TV and arrests of traffickers were on the news. I heard co-workers, family, and the public make comments about it in front of me—none of them knew I was a victim or a survivor. Some had compassionate comments and some didn't. How could I contribute to these conversations without coming out of the closet? How could I go on pretending nothing had happened to me in the past. I couldn't contribute to the anti-human trafficking conversations in an honest way if I was going to continue to hide the fact that I am a survivor. It felt like I was trying to cover up my past and going back to "keeping up appearances" again. That didn't sit right with me. I simply had to "come out of the closet" and get into the anti-human trafficking movement. I have so much to offer those who are trapped, and to the advocates who walk alongside them.

Now my life has come full circle. *Now* I can say it's a life well lived. That voice inside me tells me I'm doing the right thing. The beauty of life is, while we can't undo what is done, we can see it, understand it, learn from it, and change.

When one can clearly see their blessings, can clearly see the truth they couldn't see before, it's hard to be quiet. The abuse had taught me to be complacent and to be quiet—all that has changed.

I have a voice and I'm going to use it.

EDUCATE • EMPOWER • FREE VICTIMS

In 2016, I co-authored this enlightening eLearning program with Certified Speaking Professional and best-selling author, Patti Hathaway. Check it out and let me know if you are interested in learning more about how to bring this to your healthcare organization. We can certainly adapt this content to meet the needs of other professionals who encounter HT victims in their work. Please let us know how we can serve you!

Human Trafficking Awareness for Healthcare: W.A.R. on Slavery is a three-minute-a-day program for educating your staff on how to recognize and engage with trafficking victims. Its 20 lessons provide gripping real-life victim stories that will change the mindsets and hearts of your team to utilize the tools and action steps so they can help victims escape their slavery. In this program, your staff will learn:

- Warmth and Protection keys that are essential to connecting and providing a safe haven for human trafficking victims;
- Assessment tool for recognizing "red flags" and working with victims utilizing a 4-step process;
- Releasing shame and blame from victims by understanding the victim mentality and brainwashing tactics of pimps and others who enslave these victims.

A tri-fold printable Learning Aid pdf is provided to assist staff in remembering the key points and action strategies (available on our website). For FREE access to our first 3 lessons, go to www.HumanTraffickingeLearning.com

Abolitionist William Wilberforce once said, "You may choose to look the other way but you can never say again that you did not know. Let it not be said that I was silent when they needed me."

89292638R00103

Made in the USA
Lexington, KY
25 May 2018